A Sporting Year in Maine

Tom Roth

A Sporting Year in Maine

Copyright © 2021 by Tom Roth

All rights reserved. No part of this book may be reproduced or transmitted in any form or by any means without written permission of the author.

ISBN 978-1-943424-66-5

LCCN 2021937347

Illustrations by Barry Julius and Kelly Reissfelder

Photos by Tom Roth

North Country Press
Unity, Maine

Acknowledgments

To start, I owe a special thanks to my parents, who unfortunately did not live long enough to see this book come to fruition. My dad introduced me to the outdoors at an early age and our fishing and hunting trips were epic, at least for a youngster. Whether it was chasing pheasants that we stocked, fishing off the north pier on Lake Michigan in Sheboygan, Wisconsin (Dad's hometown), or catching salmon and smallmouth bass on Lake Sunapee, New Hampshire, or rowing the shoreline of Rangeley Lake, or finally fishing from the family places on Sebago Lake or the coast of Florida, I couldn't get enough time on the water or in the woods. We stayed close and fished every spring and summer as I grew up, and I truly believe our time in a boat played a major role in our healthy relationship. A lot was discussed while waiting for a bite or having a snack by the trunk of Dad's car after a bird hunt.

Mom pitched in when Dad was on the water with one of his buddies, watching me closely as I paced back and forth on the dock with a Zebco 33 reel on a small rod trying for bass or sunfish or whatever I could catch. A real tomboy, Mom could bait a hook and take a fish off the line, so I was in good company. She could also cook a delicious pheasant roast.

Both encouraged my writing. Bette would clip out my articles and save them, and Jerry would pore over each monthly column. He also saved clippings that he thought might serve me for future columns or interest me. I especially liked the fishing reports from Florida.

My maternal grandfather, Pa, was often along on our fishing trips and vacations, and I loved fishing with him and hearing the stories of angling past. I'm certain that the black and white photo featured in this book of Pa on a dock watching me hold up a tiny fish as a 20-month-old is a photo of the first fish I ever caught. I found the picture after my parents had passed, so I never got to ask. Knowing my mother, I'm sure she took that picture to record the auspicious event, knowing somehow her son was destined to become a devout angler.

The author's late father, Jerry Roth, with Luke. Tom credits much of his love of the outdoors and how that shaped him to his father and mother.

While my initial outdoor training was provided by family, my "graduate studies" came the way of a supervisor who would become a good friend and lifelong outdoor companion. It was 1988 and I had graduated from the University of Maine and I landed a job at the Auburn Police Department. I was truly wet behind the ears, and a salty veteran found out the new guy liked to hunt and fish, so he arranged to have me assigned to his shift. Rene "The Mouse" Lavoie was a 47-year-old lieutenant who spent his spare time roaming the woods and waters from Sebago Lake to the Rangeley region, as well as the coast and other spots in between. Working the same shift, we enjoyed the same days off, so it wasn't long before we were getting in some memorable hunting and fishing experiences. That was more than 30 years ago, and you'll get a chance to relive some of these memories with me and learn more about The Mouse.

Rene Lavoie served as the author's police supervisor, mentor, and friend and will appear throughout this book, mostly in humorous veins.

When you tag along with someone in the outdoors, you learn things their way and experience their interests. Rene loved trolling for salmon and trout when the ice left the lakes and that soon became my interest as well. Before social media and cell phones, we would have to call other anglers or drive around checking the area lakes, watching for ice-out. Lake Auburn was easy. We would drive around the lake while on patrol and could easily guess when the ice would be out enough to fish it. Likewise, when we worked night shift, we would check the brooks flowing in and out of the lake for black clouds of smelt to time the run just right. Lake Auburn was and still is closed to smelting, so I'm sure we angered a few game wardens who were hiding in the cold April woods watching for poachers.

After spending 30 years in close proximity to someone, be it in a canoe, a duck blind, a camp or an ice shack, you learn their ways and they learn yours. You can anticipate their moves and they yours. That's the type of relationship we enjoy, and I'm proud to say we never had a spat or argument on any of our ventures. That's not to say we didn't enjoy some good-natured ribbing, but I'll save that for the coming chapters. Rene nicknamed me "Towhead" because when I started on the force, I had blond hair. Rene's nickname was "Mouse" after the cartoon character, Mighty Mouse who, like Rene, was strong and tenacious.

Will Lund, editor of *The Maine Sportsman*, along with his dad, Jon, who owns the publication, have been gracious enough to keep me on over the years. I even get to meet many of our readers at their annual State of Maine Sportsman's Show in Augusta, so their support and feedback are much appreciated. I'm also honored that Will agreed to write the foreword and edit this book.

Although I met him only once, Ralph "Bud" Leavitt is the real inspiration for this book. Bud was a newspaper columnist and the Outdoor Editor for the *Bangor Daily News* and his column ran from 1948 until 1994, when he passed. In 1986, while I was majoring in Wildlife Management at the University of Maine at Orono, my college advisor suggested I apply for a scholarship given by the New England Outdoor Writers Association. Bud conducted the interviews, and I had a chance to chat with this larger-than-life personality. While I didn't get the scholarship, I did make it a point to get Bud's book, *Twelve Months in Maine*, and that was the inspiration for this book. My aim is not to duplicate Leavitt's 1977 work, but to provide an updated compendium of the sporting opportunities this great state has to offer. I hope Bud enjoys my attempt.

Finally, I am proud and honored to have the illustrations in this book done by renowned wildlife artist, Barry Julius. Barry is an award-winning artist who has the honor of having several pieces of his work featured on Massachusetts waterfowl and other hunting license stamps. Additionally, Kelly Reissfelder graciously provided two much-needed, last-minute illustrations. With that, let's push forward. We have a whole year to take on.

Apologies

Anyone who knows me well knows these simple facts: I don't like to be wrong. I say it like it is and I will apologize if I am incorrect. In that vein, let me begin by apologizing to readers in advance.

The terms used in the book, including names of popular flies or lures, places, or fishing and hunting terms are ones I have heard and picked up over the years. Because so many of my sporting pals have hailed from the Lewiston/Auburn and Sebago Lake region, there may be variations in use or exact term. A fish-finder rig at Dag's Bait Shop in Auburn might be called a sliding sinker rig at Indian Hill Trading Post in Greenville.

While I penned this book in such a way that my daughters can read it proudly, I may weave in an off-color word or two in order to provide a true account of what transpired. Some of my stories are not suitable for dinner table discussions, but that's what makes them funny to my ear. If you are easily offended, my sincere apologies.

In my 25 years as a regional columnist with *The Maine Sportsman*, I have heard this phrase countless times: "Don't go writing about our fishing/hunting trip and be so specific that everyone knows where to go." Our instructions from the editors have been to cover the region adequately so that a neophyte can go out and enjoy some of the success we enjoy. My goal was also to detail the techniques that work for me in my home waters and woods in hopes that others find they work where they fish or hunt.

Some anglers get mad when I praise Lake Auburn as a good salmon lake, fearing I will invite hordes of anglers to "their private spot" and ruin the fishing. I have not witnessed any onslaught of traffic directly attributable to my columns. In fact, I have noticed a general decline in the number of hunters and anglers in the woods and on the waters. I have attempted to cover my region, provide some how-to, where-to and when-to without giving away too many secrets. If I speak too well of your favorite fishing or hunting spot, my apologies. If you found a small kernel of wisdom in my prose, you're welcome.

My goal in the coming pages is to paint a picture for the reader of what a typical year in Maine is like for the average angler and hunter, month by month. I'll throw in a little how-to in the hopes that these tips may help you someday, whether you recreate in Maine or elsewhere. I'll weave in a few humorous incidents, as well. I can promise you that every line in this book happened as I describe. The events in these stories and any resemblance to real events or living persons is intentional.

I'm done explaining things. Let's get on to the meat and potatoes.

Foreword

By Will Lund
Editor, *The Maine Sportsman*

Simply put, Tom Roth is the real deal, and in the pages of *A Sporting Year in Maine* that follow, he takes us through each month of the calendar, telling true stories from his years of experience in the woods and fields, and on the waters and ice, of our great state.

As a college student in Orono, Tom and his like-minded friends hunted in nearby towns between classes. As a young police officer in Auburn, he looked forward to courtroom cases settling so he could make good use of a few hours left in the afternoon.

And Tom has the rare ability to place his stories in context – he correctly sees his outdoor experiences as part of a continuum initiated by his grandparents and parents, who taught him how to operate boats, handle a rod and reel, and eventually use (and later instruct others on the safe use of) firearms.

No arm-chair sportsman, Tom provides details that come only from being there – specific lures, flies and gear; shotguns in .410, 20, 16 and 12 gauge; deer and moose and bear (and even caribou); ruffed grouse, pheasant, scoters and long-tail ducks.

To paraphrase a popular slogan, "He *knows* a thing or two, because he's *seen* a thing or two."

And although Tom has an appreciation of the way things used to be done, he's far from a luddite who limits himself to the gear and techniques of a bygone era. Rather, he is equally comfortable discussing under-ice fish-locating sonar, battery-powered ice augers and electric downriggers integrated to depth-finders.

Along the way, Tom shares practical knowledge, instructing without lecturing – maintaining an antique outboard motor; waiting for whitetail deer where forest meets clearing; field-dressing a moose; and reducing risks while participating in the challenging sport of sea duck hunting.

Tom takes us through a calendar year, frequently reminding us to enjoy each day outdoors even as we anticipate and plan for the coming season.

This book is clearly a labor of love for Tom, and it shows. The reader is along for the ride with the author, his constant companion Rene, and Tom's chocolate lab, Luke.

As Tom's editor at *The Maine Sportsman* magazine, where he's provided regional columns for more than 20 years, I've had the opportunity to get to know Tom, and it's clear why his writings have appeared in national magazines. This book has allowed him to go beyond a single story or article and think back on his lifetime of outdoors adventures. It's a thank-you note to every relative, friend, co-worker and hunting dog that's accompanied him and helped him develop into the truly well-rounded hunter and angler he is today.

And every tale is true. As Tom himself asserts, events in his stories are real, and any resemblance to actual persons is intentional.

Enjoy!

Table of Contents

January 1
February 16
March 22
April 27
May 40
June 60
July 68
August 75
September 84
October 97
November 124
December 135
A Traveling Sportsman 141
Boats and Motors 157
At Camp 164
On Dogs 169
The Big Lake 174
Tidying Up 179

January

Hard Water Angling Begins

Pulling up the collar on my wool coat, I trudge toward the lake, pulling a plastic tote sled with all my essentials for the day. The cold wind bites at my cheeks and takes my breath away. The sweat starting to form on the back of my neck feels like it will freeze and causes me to shiver.

Once at my favorite spot, I pull the cord on the ice auger, one I've owned for more than 25 years, and it springs to life. Proper care, good fuel and a fresh spark plug each season pays off. With the first hole drilled, I scoop out the slush and get my trap ready. I'm targeting trout, so I use my small traps that end with six feet of eight-pound test leader and a number six hook. I shove my bare hand into the bait bucket and pull out a small, lively shiner, hook it just behind the dorsal fin and drop it into the water.

Four more holes are drilled and, by now, my jacket is hanging over my auger and the cold wind is evaporating my sweat. My fingers are cracked from exposure to the icy waters and I fumble around in my pack basket for the thermos. A piping hot cup of coffee feels good on the hands and in my core, and I begin my vigil for the first trap to spring. This scenario has repeated itself over many years, and the stalwart feeling I get by conquering the elements draws me back each season.

Rene tends his ice fishing trap.

It used to be that January 1st heralded the official start of ice fishing season. Checking the local ponds that were frozen was a good gauge to determine which of your friends had celebrated too strenuously the night before, as evidenced by their absence. Now, you can pretty much ice fish on any water once it freezes in my part of the state. That's too early, in my humble opinion, as I still haven't put away my deer hunting gear, but die-hard ice anglers rejoice this law change.

Maine winters are long, and if you don't enjoy some form of outdoor recreation you will likely suffer depression from shortened daylight hours, gain winter weight and quite possibly go stir crazy. Ice fishing, while not on par with snowshoeing or cross-country skiing in terms of calorie-burners, can suffice. Sprinting to a sprung trap when someone yells "Flag!" is great exercise. So is drilling a hole through three feet of ice. Of course, you burn more calories if you employ a hand auger, but I have seen some anglers work up quite a sweat just attempting to pull-start their old two-stroke augers.

Ice angling in my home region takes on several forms. First there are trips to local ponds for trout, as soon as the ice is safe. These are punctuated by trips to the coastal rivers to target smelt–delicious to eat and great for bait used later in the season. Finally, when the larger lakes freeze, I spend my time on the ice for lake trout and salmon or the somewhat new pike. Let's start with a trip to one of my favorite trout haunts, my early January go-to spot, the Range (pronounced "rang") Ponds.

The Range Ponds (Lower, Middle and Upper) in Poland freeze relatively early, have plenty of access points and are stocked with three of the common trout species we see in Maine: brook trout, rainbows, and browns. Additionally, the state puts in enough brood stock whoppers to make the fishing exciting. These are large, mature fish used for hatchery breeding.

Adam Farrington and proud son Connor show off a lovely Range Pond brown trout.

January

Southern Maine has many ponds and small lakes that are stocked with one or more of the trout species, and the techniques I use on the Range Pond chain will work on any of them.

Staying within this region's five-trap legal limit, I typically begin my day as the sun hits the pond and drill a series of holes beginning right at the shoreline (targeting brook trout), working my way out to deeper water. I also drill a hole in about 12 to 18 feet of water to use for jigging.

For brookies, I like a gob of worms on the hook set in shallow water. Some anglers report catching fish in mere inches of water, but I fish in three or four feet so I can get my trap under the ice.

Moving deeper, I use small shiners, setting a few close to the bottom and some midway up the water column. Once I start to get bites, I'll move all my lines to the preferred depth.

The ice-angler's tools of the trade.

When jigging for trout, small jigs like the Thomas Buoyant or Al's Goldfish work wonders. I find gold, orange and brook trout patterns work best.

January

Middle Range Pond offers the greatest variety of the three and seems to be the favorite among Lewiston/Auburn sportsmen and women. For many years, healthy doses of brookies were poured into the water in anticipation of creating a great, nearby brook trout fishery. The pond features a maximum depth of 66 feet. Several brooks feed into the pond and combine with underground springs to guarantee top trout conditions. Check the Maine Department of Inland Fisheries and Wildlife (DIF&W) website for their regularly updated stocking report. Chances are there is a small pond near you that receives regular doses of fish. Be sure to go back in the reports a few years and look for stocking trends.

While primary stocking efforts varied between brook trout and brown trout, stocking reports for the last decade show that Middle Range Pond is receiving more and more rainbow trout. Small shiners fished just off bottom in the shallows are perhaps the best way to fish for Middle Range 'bows. These colorful fish often fall to shiny jigging spoons or worms, too.

For a great eating fish, I target Middle and Upper Range Pond for white perch. These distant cousins of the striped bass are abundant and always seem to be on the bite. Anglers report excellent success on the lower end of Middle Range Pond in 40 feet of water. Small shiners and worms work well for those pursuing this hearty chowder fish.

While Middle Range Pond is one of the busiest spots in the winter, anglers should not overlook Upper Range, especially when after brown trout. Anglers fishing the shallows on the east shore around the boat launch do well. I find brown trout to be the most finicky fish to catch through the ice. Small shiners, light leaders and minimal disturbance around the hole pay dividends when targeting brownies. Try these techniques on your favorite pond early this season.

We often forget how much has changed with technology and access to waters. I had a chance to fish a remote lake, Lobster Lake above Greenville, named for its resemblance to an actual lobster. My roommate, George Belmont's dad, Sonny, supervised the Lobster Lake operation for the old Great Northern Paper

Company. With that position came a company four-wheel-drive truck with a two-way radio. This was long before cell phones and was a godsend in the northern woods for safety's sake. Family members were allowed to drive the truck and gas was paid for by the company.

Adam Farrington (left) and Rene Lavoie with a nice Upper Range Pond rainbow trout.

The woodcutters at the Lobster Lake camp were mostly Canadians and would leave to go home on the weekends. We had access to the camp bunks, the company truck with gas and an old Ski-Doo sled. What more could a crew of college kids need? To sweeten the pot, the camp cook even left us food! I don't recall

January

what we all caught for fish, but I do remember Lobster Lake had some decent salmon in it. I also remember the moist and sweet chocolate cake the camp cook left for us to enjoy.

Winter Smelting

January angling for smaller prey can be equally exciting. When the coastal rivers freeze and the commercial smelt shacks are hauled onto the ice by tractors and four-wheelers, it's time to call for a reservation, and fish a tide on a blustery winter's night.

Smelt shacks dot the coastal rivers and estuaries like the Kennebec River and Merrymeeting Bay and its tributaries, and I have visited most of them from Bowdoinham to Randolph. If you haven't tried winter smelting, you should, as it is quite an experience from many angles.

To begin with, most smelt camp owners are colorful characters. I'm not sure why, but it's just the way it is. A typical smelt operation requires you to drive down an icy dirt road to a cramped parking spot. Once there, you gather your belongings from the truck and hike to the office. Typically, the office is an old camper with yellow walls from years of cigarette smoke and slippery linoleum from anglers' boots. You pay the proprietor the fee that covers one tide and get a bag of blood worms, the ugliest things you will ever see, along with the general direction to your shack.

These shacks are another thing. Every engineering style is evident and siding and roof choices are testimony to human ingenuity. The most comfortable shacks have electric lights and some form of heat. I prefer wood heat just because there is something old-fashioned about keeping a wood stove stoked all night. If the stove has a flat top, I always bring along a chowder or baked beans to heat up for a midnight snack.

Last year we had our best feed yet. I brought along lobster stew and a baguette that I warmed in foil and topped with a large hunk of butter. Big pieces of lobster and a hint of sherry provided some five-star dining in our little piece of heaven on the Kennebec River. On some nights, I'll pack sandwiches and warm them on

January

the stove. Rene opts for more simple fare and typically brings a salmon sandwich or a tin of sardines and some crackers.

I don't imbibe when angling and neither does my usual partner, Rene, a devout teetotaler, but it seems everyone else on the river does. You can almost keep track of the passage of time by the volume of your neighbor's hoots and hollers as their drinking increases with each passing hour. Shacks on the ice are placed mere feet from one another so there is no privacy. It's not uncommon to hear what sounds like rain hitting your shack but I can assure you it's not raining on a single-digit January night. I have heard arguments over items dropped down the race hole, stories of missed shots at deer, and I'm pretty sure I heard a couple attempting to conceive a child, all while I was smelting snug in my rented shack.

Rene and I opt for a four-man shack just because it gives us enough room to maneuver. All shacks come with "house lines" typically consisting of a series of six or so heavy cod lines wrapped around wooden dowels drilled into a piece of lumber attached toward the roof of the shack. The lines end with a leader and a heavy sinker, tipped with a tiny hook. There will be a blood-stained wooden plank in the shack. Don't be alarmed, it's not evidence of an ice shack homicide. It's used to slice up your bloodworm to bait the hook.

Rene and I forego the house lines and use our own smelt jigs. We use small, springy rods with built-in plastic spool reels and run one-pound test line. A small dart-type jig is baited with a tiny piece of bloodworm, and the wait begins. Depending on how fast the action is, I may employ up to four rods.

When the smelt are on the bite, I can barely tend to one rod. Hovering over the hole, I watch the spring tip of the rod for any sign of activity. If the line bounces at all, you must quickly pick up the rod and set the hook. When set shallow, you can pull the line up high and get the smelt out of the water. When running deeper, you have to reel your prize in.

January

Saltwater smelt, the same species as our freshwater smelt, is actually the rainbow smelt, *Osmerus mordax*. Salters, as they are often called, run from a few inches up to a foot or so. I prefer the small ones, say five to seven inches. It doesn't take many to make a good feed, but on a good night you can catch a hundred or more, but be sure to abide by the limit. In the region I described, anglers can keep four quarts of smelt.

The silver-sided rainbow smelt provides hours of angling fun on a cold winter's night.

January

A simple way to measure four quarts is to fill a white pail half full of water and mark that point with a permanent marker. Now add four quarts of water and mark that line. When you start fishing, fill your bucket with river water up to the bottom line. Add your smelts as you catch them and when the water reaches the top line, you have four quarts. Simple.

Cleaning and cooking these delicacies is easy, too. After a night on the ice, I hover over the kitchen sink with cold running water. I snip the heads off the fish and then run the scissors down the body cavity, cutting down through the vent. (Vent is a more appetizing way of saying anus.) I then run my thumb down the body and expel the innards, while using my nail to scrape the spleen away from the top inside of the fish. I rinse the whole fish clean and then dry it on a paper towel.

Once it's time to cook them, I simply dredge them in flour that has been seasoned with salt and pepper. Sometimes I use cornmeal seasoned in the same manner. Slip the fish into a high-sided pan filled with an inch or so of vegetable oil, and fry on both sides until golden brown. Serve hot with tartar sauce and you have the makings of a grand smelt feed.

Snowshoe Hare Hunting

I put my shotgun away at the close of bird season, but if someone invites me on a winter-time hare hunt, I jump at the chance. Many years ago, Rene and I had a friend with a pair of beagles and when snow conditions were just right, we enjoyed many a rabbit hunt. I love watching any hunting dog work their quarry, but it's almost comical to watch a pot-bellied beagle howling and trying to keep up with a fast-moving snowshoe hare.

On one memorable hunt, I was carrying my favorite hare shotgun, my grandfather's single-shot .410 Lefever. This was the first gun I owned, and the agreement my grandfather had with my parents was when I was mature enough to own a gun, he would give it to me. I think that shotgun kept me from getting into more trouble than I will ever know. The story behind how my grandfather got it was equally as enthralling.

My grandfather lived on the family farm during the Depression, and he told me that a man needed food for his family, so Pa traded him three rabbits he had shot for the shotgun. I recall asking Pa why the man didn't use the shotgun to kill his own food, but Pa didn't have the answer. I honed my shooting skills targeting squirrels with that .410. It made the perfect gun for rabbits, as it was lightweight and shot true with its full choke.

Rene and I were hunting one crisp January day when the conditions were just right; there were a few inches of snow, crusted over with ice and a dusting of new snow on top of that. The bunnies were running but we couldn't seem to intercept them. We didn't have radio collars or tracking units like so many hunters use today, so we had to rely on gauging the sound of the baying beagles to decide on an ambush spot.

As I loaded up my .410, it went off as I closed the hinge action. Because gun safety was ingrained in me at an early age, aided by the fact that I was a police firearms instructor for close to 20 years, I had the shotgun pointed in a safe direction and any mishap was avoided. I repeated the process and the gun discharged again. Rene, an instructor and armorer looked my little shotgun over and declared the firing pin was either elongated or was sticking. I held the lever open as I closed it and that solved the problem. Needless to say, I was more than cautious with that gun for the rest of the hunt (turns out the action needed cleaning, which was a quick fix when I got it home).

Without any shots being fired, we were getting bored and Rene started poking fun at my diminutive, malfunctioning shotgun. Not one to be toyed with when it comes to a family heirloom, I told him that if he wanted to throw his piss-pot of a hat up in the air, I'd show him how good my gun was. He removed the green wool hat that likely arrived with the Mayflower and spun it high into the air. I let the hat reach its apex and fired. When he retrieved it, I had drilled a one-inch hole through the wool with my tight choked Lefever. I was content with my shooting, even though I didn't take a rabbit that day.

Chasing bunnies across the January countryside is fun and a good workout to boot. Snowshoes aid hunters when the snow gets deeper, but snow too deep or powdery will spell an end to the beagles being deployed. Of course, you can hunt the thickets for hare without a dog, but I doubt you will be as successful. Speaking of dogs, they require and deserve a little extra time during the cold winter months.

Winter Dog Care

We can't forget our faithful companions just because the guns and gear of fall's hunting season are put away. Whether you live in Maine or any other part of the country that sees winter, this time of year is harsh on humans and can be brutal on even the most stalwart dog. By preparing your companion for the approaching weather, you can ensure that he remains healthy and strong enough to take on the coming year's hunting season.

Perhaps the most important consideration of wintertime pet care is nutrition. While your dog may have required extra feed and extra protein during the previous hunting season, most dogs, like their owners, slow down in the wintertime. Just as the winter doldrums keep us indoors and reduce our level of activity, the same happens with most pets, especially those kept inside. A dog accustomed to running itself ragged in the field that suddenly finds himself inside next to the fireplace doesn't know enough to reduce his caloric intake. We must take that upon ourselves to do.

At the recommendation of my vet, I fed my Lab two cups of food in the morning and two cups of food in the evening. During hunting season, I up that to three cups at each feeding, to maintain his weight around 70 pounds. As soon as the last shotgun is oiled and put away in the gun cabinet, I go back to the two-cup limit. Those hunters who switch their dog food to one with a higher protein content during the working season must also wean their dogs back to the standard fare, come winter. It's important to

January

remember, however, that dogs kept outside in the winter may need more food to stay warm. It pays to consult your vet on that issue.

Once your favorite companion is set up with a proper diet, it is imperative to remember that water is equally as important to their health. While dehydration is a common problem in the summer months, it can and does occur in the winter months. Although it is not a problem for the inside dog, dogs kept outdoors or in unheated kennels need access to unfrozen water. The best solution for that problem is a water heater. While these devices don't really heat the water to a scalding temperature, they do manage to keep the water ice-free. It is important to pick a quality brand that protects the dog, and owner, from electric shock. The better models have protected elements and heavy cords that are shielded to prevent chewing by inquisitive pups.

Once you have satisfied your pet's need for food and water, it only follows that you put some thought into their shelter. For the indoor dog, that may consist of a cedar-filled bed next to your favorite easy chair, or perhaps the luxury of an old couch to soothe their tired bones.

The outdoor dog is a bit more of a challenge. For some pups, a dog house is the only shelter they may get when the wind howls out of the north. If that is the case, be sure the opening to the house is positioned out of the way of the prevailing winds. You may also want to insulate the house for the winter months.

Your other consideration should be bedding. I prefer hay because it is easy to work with, inexpensive, and easy to clean. If you choose hay, be certain it is dry. No one likes sleeping in a wet bed, especially when the mercury drops. Some kennel owners prefer wood shavings. These give a similar amount of warmth as hay and are also easy to manage. For those living in extremely cold environments, an effective kennel/dog house heater can be made using an ordinary light bulb. By wiring a lamp fixture near the top of the kennel, and safely protecting it from fire hazards, you can easily warm the area from the radiant heat of the bulb. Plans for such a device are often included in many of the popular dog training books. Today, pressure-activated heating pads add a great deal of warmth and protection for an outside dog.

Once the rudimentary needs of food, water and shelter are met, it's time to move on to grooming. First and foremost are the toenails, especially if your dog is going to venture out in the snow and onto the ice. Nothing can rip a nail off your dog's feet quicker than running on jagged ice. Keep the nails trimmed so that they don't make clicking noises when they run on a hard floor. While you can pay the vet for this service, it is easy to learn and can prolong your dog's comfort, especially when spending time outdoors during the snow season.

It is equally important to keep the hair on the dog's foot pads neatly trimmed, as snow and ice can accumulate between the digits and cause painful cuts or even frozen pads. Some hair is necessary for insulation, but too much only attracts problems.

Coat maintenance is also a difficult task in the winter. While most dogs, especially the water breeds, get plenty of baths in the summer and fall, most owners don't bathe or swim their dogs in the winter. No one wants a wet dog shaking in the house, but a lack of regular bathing can cause skin problems and coat odor. If you bathe Fido in the winter, be certain that he is dry before sending him outside. A thick towel and even a hair dryer, if your dog will tolerate it, will even dry the heavy-coated breeds.

Winter is also a great time to get to the vet for preventative maintenance. A post-season checkup can identify minor injuries and assure you that all vaccinations are up to date. It's also a good time to have the dog's teeth cleaned if you haven't done so yet. Tooth and gum disease are leading causes of other problems in dogs and must be prevented.

Just because you have prepared your dog for winter, it doesn't mean that he must stay indoors and wait out the season. Daily exercise is important, and a romp in the snow is great for building the lungs and muscles. Most dogs love snow and winter sports like ice fishing, cross-country skiing and snowshoeing—great activities to invite your dog along on. My Lab, Luke, loved to ride on my snowmobile with me. He would much rather go along than stay at home by the fire. He would sit in front of me on the seat and gas tank, and my passengers had to stand and hold on to my tow-behind sled.

Just as your car must be prepared for the coming winter, so must your hunting dog. A little time spent now can pay big dividends when next season rolls around. By following these tips and consulting with your veterinarian, you can rest assured that the winter will be comfortable and healthy for your four-legged hunting partner.

Cold Water

Quite a number of years ago, a now-retired state trooper friend, who shall go unnamed, invited Rene and me to ice-fish near his house. We loaded up our gear, bought a few dozen shiners and headed up to his place to meet him and another trooper. On the way, the bait bucket tipped over in the bed of my truck and when we got to his house, I told him I needed some water fast. He didn't have a faucet in his basement, so he pointed to the stairs and told me I could fill the bucket at the kitchen sink. I went to the sink and turned cold water on to fill up my bait bucket. I could hear a shower running in what appeared to be the bathroom just off of the kitchen. After a few seconds, I heard a shriek and an un-clothed lady flung the bathroom door open and scolded who she thought was her husband for turning on the faucet and making her shower run hot. Upon realizing her mistake, she retreated into the bathroom. I never spoke a word and passed my friend on the stairs as I took my bait back to the truck. Once my friend returned he simply said, "I see you met my wife." I don't recall if we caught any fish that day but I can recall that awkward moment in the kitchen like it was yesterday.

As the first page of the calendar gets turned to another month, ice anglers pick up the pace. Most all our watery destinations are now safe to fish and this angler comes into his own.

February

Fishing the Big Lake for Big Togue

After I fired up my antique Ski-Doo, my faithful companion Luke climbed onto the seat to wait for me. Rene took his place standing on the dogsled attached to the machine. We zoomed out to my shack, the first one I owned, and I unlocked it. Rene went in and used the newspaper, kindling and wood I kept stored inside to get a fire going in the old water heater that was now a woodstove.

I busied myself drilling holes for traps around the shack on Sebago's Jordan Bay. By February, the lake was safe with at least a foot of good, clear ice. Once the holes were drilled and scooped out, I went in the shack and drilled two jigging holes. I walked in one direction setting four traps, and Rene went about the same task in the opposite direction. In no time we were back in the shack, jackets hung, enjoying the first cup of coffee of the morning.

I bought this shack from Milton McCabe, my neighbor in North Auburn, for $75 in 1990. It was framed with one-by-ones and was covered in the old printing tin from the *Lewiston Sun Journal*. I'm not sure when the four-by-eight-foot shack was built, but as I recall the print that was visible on the inside of the shack was from 1983. Many area shacks were covered in this lightweight

February

metal which, if you knew someone at the paper, could be had for free. The woodstove, as mentioned earlier, was an old water heater with a flat piece of metal at the top that was used as a cooking platform.

I always liked to cook in the shack, so I made breakfast sandwiches for Rene and me that would rival those sold by that orange-haired clown. Luke pushed his way into the shack to get a scrap of Canadian bacon but soon found it too warm inside and was off to explore the ice.

I went outside and removed the skim of ice from the holes where my traps were set and drilled another hole closer to shore to jig. Luke drank from the hole when it was clear of slush. Choosing my favorite lure, the Swedish pimple, I sweetened it with a piece of shiner tail. I dropped the line to the bottom and then reeled up slightly to bounce the jig inches from the base of the lake.

After a few minutes I had thoughts of moving to another hole when a big tug answered my upward twitch of the lure. I set the hook deep and began reeling the jig toward the surface. The heavy-shouldered fish pumped at each revolution of the reel, fighting my pull. A big bubble appeared in the ice hole and, before long, I hoisted my prize out of the lake—a hefty three-pound lake trout.

Sebago Lake, the scene of the aforementioned narrative, holds special interest to me. My parents summered on its shoreline and I had instant access to the big, clear lake all year round. The comfort of coming in from the cold, be it winter or spring, and warming up by the fire just a few steps from the water, can't be measured. I sure have a ton of memories fishing Sebago with my dad, but he was always in Florida during the winter. So, the Roth camp became ice-fishing central for me and my buddies, and typically by February, we had plenty of ice. Although I like setting up camp at a fixed shack and setting traps, I always had better luck moving about. I wrote about my favorite fishing technique, and my system appeared in many angling publications.

February

Jigging-on-the-Move for Togue

Ice fishermen of the past would not recognize the equipment used by today's angler. Our sporting ancestors were content to trudge through miles of forest, with snowshoes and pack basket, just to reach a hidden pond or lake. Because of the effort it took to reach their spot and chisel a hole, they tended to stay in one area, fish or no fish.

In contrast, the modern angler has a host of technological advancements at his fingertips designed to make his sport easier and more productive. Recently, jig fishermen have capitalized on these advancements and adapted the technique of "jigging-on-the-move" to cover more water and go to where the fish are.

Several seasons ago, while fishing for lake trout, I began using the technique of jigging-on-the-move. By day's end, I had caught and released over a dozen fish, including some decent ones. Now I firmly believe that by following a few techniques and using the equipment that technology has brought us, we can better utilize our time and effort on the ice.

This angler has a portable fish-finder and can move from spot to spot until he locates fish, by jigging on the move.

February

The first step in properly fishing a lake or pond is to research that body of water to find likely spots to set up. While some anglers are content to drop a line wherever convenient, they are relying on luck rather than skill, often ignoring the bottom structure and terrain that hold fish. Sedentary anglers may spend all day in one barren spot without so much as a nibble. Researching a lake solves that dilemma. A quick trip to the local bait or tackle shop will often yield clues as to where the fish are being caught. Ask specific questions of the proprietor such as what depth the fish are being taken at and what lures are being used. Numerous social media sites now provide great up-to-the-minute information on ice conditions and fishing action. I belong to several of these Maine sporting groups. Game wardens and fisheries biologists are also excellent sources for ice-fishing information. They usually know easy access points to the lakes, which can be major assets in winter.

Once you've decided on a spot to begin fishing, the use of an electronic fish-finding device greatly improves your chances of landing a fish. By drilling a "scout hole" and placing your fish-finder in it, you can immediately tell how deep the water is, what the bottom looks like and even if there are any fish below the hole.

Fish-finders that show the actual bottom and indicate fish with fish shapes or outlines work just like the electronics on our boats. Electronic flashers use the same sonar technology and indicate the depth and they show fish activity by differing color bands. Finally, underwater cameras show the angler exactly how the bottom appears and shows a real-time video of any fish cruising nearby. Anglers after schooling fish such as white perch or crappie will also benefit from the electronic fish-finder. By drilling a scout hole and using the side-viewing feature, you can often locate a school of fish under the ice. Sometimes moving your spot by as little as 50 feet may make all the difference in the world.

Merely owning an electronic fish-finder does not guarantee success for the winter angler. You must know how to properly operate it and interpret the display screen. What may appear as a rock or stump to some might actually be a fish on the bottom. By

February

thoroughly reading the instruction manual and experimenting on the ice, you should be able to differentiate between fish and bottom structure in no time. When in doubt, however, assume the object is a fish, and try jigging there for a while.

Often, you won't see a fish on the sonar, but by jigging and bouncing bottom, you may draw one in. This is especially true of the bottom-dwelling species like togue. If you don't detect a strike after 15 minutes, it's time to move on. However, if you do catch a fish right off, stay put. There may be more than one lurking in the depths.

Several years ago, I was targeting salmon on Moosehead Lake. The action was slow, so I pulled one of my traps and decided to jig for lakers. I caught six trout, some weighing several pounds each, from that same hole in less than 20 minutes. The bottom must have been crawling with them!

When you manage to locate a honey hole like that, or wish to spend more time in one area, the portable ice shack is the fisherman's dream come true. The portable ice shack of today not only combines wind-blocking strength with light weight, but they are also very affordable.

On cold and windy days, I pull a folding shack behind my snowmobile that holds all my gear. Just getting out of the breeze is often relief enough, and these shacks do provide a barrier to the biting wind. On brutally cold days, they can even be efficiently heated by a small heater or a gas lantern. Be sure to provide adequate ventilation when using an oxygen-consuming heat source such as a stove or lantern.

While some anglers prefer to set up a permanent shack for the season, the ice nomad with the portable shack can go to where the action is and still bring along the comforts of home. Nothing beats a hot meal on the ice, and cooking the traditional deer steak and beans is much easier in a pop-up shack. If you don't catch any fish, at least you will draw the envious glances from those around you who smell what you are cooking!

The power ice auger is the most energy-saving method of making holes in the ice ever to come on the market. With a mere pull of the starter cord—or the flick of a switch on the newer battery-powered augers—a lone fisherman can cut and bait five holes in the time it takes a chisel-user or hand-cranker to cut just one. These devices are designed to operate in below-zero weather with manual chokes and fuel priming buttons for ease of starting on the coldest of mornings. Battery models will work in all temperatures, but it helps if they are kept somewhat warm.

By having these tools at their disposal, the modern angler does not feel compelled to stay in one spot where his shack is or feel burdened by lugging his gear around on foot. Mobile anglers can move where the fish are—an important point when fishing large lakes or when after schooling fish.

Although technological advancements in wintertime fishing may be frowned upon by some who opt for the simpler methods, it can't be ignored that the tools we have today allow us to spend more time outdoors. By combining these tools and advancements with proper scouting and lure choice, jigging-on-the-move can produce action for the wandering angler when others are anchored to one spot on the lake.

Winter is not over when the shortest month ends. While the ice may start to get punky as warm March days bring increased sunlight, the ice is typically good on many Maine lakes for most of the month. With that thought in mind, let's turn the calendar one more page.

March

Cusk and Crow Provide Great Sport This Month

It was early in the month and mild during the day but still cold enough to make ice at night. I was working night shift and, on my days off, I found it easier on my sleep cycle if I stayed up late. On a whim I loaded up my ice fishing gear and headed to the family camp on Sebago Lake to fish for cusk. I pulled my shack off the ice a few days earlier when the holes around it started to open up, not wanting to lose it if a heat wave came in.

I got to camp and had a nice supper before heading out on the lake. I was in luck. I could use my old holes, as they were just skimmed over, but decided to set traps closer to shore where I surmised the cusk would be. Motoring out on my Ski-Doo, I cut five holes from camp along the shore toward Jordan Bay. My chocolate Lab, Luke, loved to ride on my sled but couldn't figure out what I was doing out at night. In any case, he made no bones about it and went along for the adventure. I must have been the only soul on the lake that weekday night as I couldn't see any lights or snow machines. I had been saltwater smelting a week earlier and I had a dozen smelt left over. These big smelts get mushy in the refrigerator but make ideal cusk bait, especially if they start to get pungent.

Using a lead depth sounder, I found bottom and dropped in a baited hook. I peeled off several additional feet of line and

March

watched it sink in the headlight of my idling sled. Repeating this scenario four more times, I had the legal number of traps set and I had an hour before I had to check them again.

Back at camp I lit a fire in the fireplace and settled into Dad's old recliner. With a cup of coffee and a book, I relaxed until my watch indicated an hour was up. Out we headed with high hopes.

It's amazing how direction at night changes. I always look for the radio tower on Brown Hill in Raymond when I need a point of reference for the camp. It's lit with a flashing red light to warn low-flying aircraft and it serves to direct me no matter where I am on the lake. It was erected in 1959 and at the time, it was the tallest structure in the world at 1,619 feet.

I headed toward the blinking tower and then made a hard right, finally picking up my first trap in the headlight of the old Safari 503. Nothing. Four more traps checked and no action at those, either. I motored back to the camp and settled into the warmth by the fireplace. I made five or six more trips, all with no luck. I thought Luke would eventually stay behind, but he insisted on accompanying me on each sortie.

Finally, close to 1:00 a.m. I had a flag on my second trap! I whizzed the sled over as soon as I saw the red felt flag in my light and shut the machine down as Luke jumped off, sensing something was afoot. I used my small flashlight to look at the spool of the trap and saw that it sat motionless. However, the line was off to the side of the hole. Normally I would wait for the fish to swim, but I know cusk will swallow their prey and sit while digesting it, so I pulled lightly but firmly on the line. I could feel the fish writhe and knew instantly I had my intended quarry. This one came up easily, and I was pleased to see a two-pound fish curling up on the cold ice. Luke got a nose-full of cusk odor and I slipped my prize into my pack basket. Checking the rest of the traps produced nothing, so I motored back to camp and put the fish in the sink for later.

Related to the cod, the cusk or *Lota*, is also referred to as a burbot, which draws its Latin meaning from "barba" or beard, likely due to the single whisker under the fish's chin. The cusk is an odd-looking fish, and I liken it to a cross between an eel and a hornpout. Whatever you think about its appearance, the cusk is a fine-eating fish, and I wanted mine for chowder.

Like its saltwater cousin, the cod, cusk are high in vitamin D-rich oil from their liver, and that organ makes up ten-percent of its body weight. That's more than six times the size of livers in other freshwater fish, in case you were curious.

Cusk move into shallow water in the winter and prefer a sandy or mucky bottom. The shallows just off the Route 302 beach in Raymond are perfect habitat for these bottom dwellers. My saltwater smelt work wonders, as do fillets from a large sucker or common shiner. I think cusk prefer dead bait over live, but that debate could go on for days.

Cusk aren't the most glamorous fish, and fishing for them isn't, either. Cold nights on the ice that blend into the early morning hours aren't always fun, but they are productive if you want a nice winter chowder. That night on Sebago I didn't catch any more cusk, but I managed to stay up late and sleep in, maintaining my night shift schedule and I caught one of the lake's unsung heroes, the lowly but delicious burbot.

Crow Hunting

Aside from hare hunting, there isn't much sport to be had in the winter months. However, crow season opens in March, and a good old-fashioned crow hunt is just the thing to hone your wing shooting skills and dump those cabin fever blues.

It was a typical mild March morning. The air temperature was in the 30s but snow was melting and it was foggy. As I drove down Route 136 from Auburn into Durham, I was looking at the cornfields, covered with snow but showing a few bare brown spots where the ground was uncovered. I parked next to a field and lugged my gear bag to the tree line as the morning sky brightened.

In a few minutes I had my crow decoys set out, remote call in place and the final touch was an owl decoy in the field. I could see black dots against the morning sky coming over the river from Lewiston, so I knew the crows were flying.

Once I was settled in among the bare trees, trying to hide against the trunk of the largest maple I could find, I loaded my shotgun and turned the call on. The raucous calling was hard to listen to, but it began to draw the birds in. First singles, then a few more. In a matter of seconds, I had a murder of crows (as a group of crows is called), circling overhead looking for the gang that wasn't there.

A few birds locked in on the lone owl decoy perched in the field. I concentrated on those. I drew a bead on the closest one and fired. It flinched but soon crumpled up and dropped at my second shot. The rest retreated and the sky was once again silent. This was crow hunting, fun and fast! A pleasant diversion on a late-winter day and a great way to hone your shooting skills for the upcoming fall.

Pulling the Shack

March is also the time to pull your shack from the ice. I waited a bit too long to remove my ice shack from Sebago Lake a number of years ago and it taught me and my friend quite a lesson. It was mid-March and we had quite a bit of mild, sunny weather. My 4 by 8 metal shack was lightweight and would fit in the bed of my truck. Two men could easily load it up and haul it away.

I enlisted the help of a non-ice fishing friend to assist. Timmy Morrell worked with me as a cop for most of our careers, so we knew each other well. We had been in a scrape or two together and now can laugh about all those memories. But Timmy was no outdoorsman, so this was new territory for him. The plan was to pull the shack ashore with my Ski-Doo and then load it into my truck and haul it home for another year. It sat just offshore from the family camp on Jordan Bay. We motored out onto the ice where my shack was tied down over 35 feet of water.

Several days and nights of thawing and freezing had anchored the runners on the bottom of the ice shack into the lake ice. We took turn chiseling around the runners until it rocked back and forth, a sure sign it was free. I hooked my sled up to the runners and my friend pushed at the back of the shack. I gunned it and my forward momentum told me it was free. I turned around just in time to see Timmy frantically waving his arms as he teetered on the edge of a hole in the ice the same size as the base of my shack. Fortunately, he didn't fall in, but the memory of that event forces me to pull my shack earlier in the month and it cured him of any interest in ice angling or shack pulling. We still laugh about this day on the ice. Well, I laugh.

The end of March traditionally heralded the start of open-water season on April 1, but now with the law changes, anglers in the southern part of the state can fish most lakes as soon as the ice is gone, with some restrictions. Nothing gets this angler as excited as ice-out, so hurry up and turn the calendar to April!

April

Ice Out Heralds the Best Salmon Fishing of the Year

The ice had just gone out on Lake Auburn, and I lived up the road from the boat launch at the time. I joked that I could pull out of my driveway and coast my truck all the way to the launch. On this day, I did just that and was on the water in no time. I motored over to aptly-named Salmon Point as the sun started to rise in front of me.

As my boat neared the point of land that marked an underwater ridge, I began to pump the fly-rod back and forth. I could picture the sparse fly attached to the leader darting ahead in the water, then pausing as if it were a crippled smelt. Surely a salmon would find this action attractive.

After perhaps six pulls on the rod, I began to wonder if there were any fish to be caught. I had diligently checked the brooks that led into my favorite lake for the past three nights, so I knew that the smelts were running strong. After jigging the rod forward one more time and letting the fly settle back, a sharp series of taps on the rod tip signaled that a fish was on. I snapped the rod tip forward and palmed the reel as the salmon made for deeper water with my fly securely anchored in its bony mouth.

I barely had time to celebrate the fact that this was my first fish on a fly this season as the salmon changed its course and broke the water with a stunning tail dance. While some would argue that a fish caught on a fly while trolling doesn't qualify as a fly-fishing prize, I beg to differ. This was traditional salmon trolling with flies, a favorite rite of spring for many Maine sportsmen and women alike and one of my favorite ways to fish.

Jerry Roth shows off a nice ice-out salmon taken while trolling on Rangeley Lake.

Trolling flies for trout is as old as fly-fishing itself. Scottish anglers of old who cast long rods with large flies out over storied rivers occasionally used boats to fish farther out on the river. Some of these sage anglers discovered that by playing out all their line and stripping it in, they could catch fish without casting, resting the sore arms that spent the whole day wrestling with 12-foot rods. It didn't take long for them to learn that they could cover more water with their flies if they paddled while the line was out in the water. Perhaps this is how the sport of trolling was born. Because of the success that trolling can bring, anglers are now prohibited from trolling flies on fly-fishing-only lakes and ponds in Maine.

Anglers in Maine have been using these techniques for as long as fly rods and canoes were present on our abundant lakes and ponds. Fly-rodders trolled their streamer flies with much success, but many felt that they needed a bigger fly, so the trolling streamer evolved from many of the original casting streamer patterns.

One of Maine's most famous fly dressers created a fly that closely resembled the smelt and earned her fame and admiration throughout New England and around the world. Carrie Stevens of Upper Dam in the Rangeley Region was a milliner, creating feathered hats that were all the rage in the 1920s. She was also the wife of noted fishing guide Wallace Stevens. As the legend goes, Carrie was doing her housework on July 1, 1924, when she had an urge to take some of the feathers she used in making her hats and create a streamer fly with gray wings to imitate a smelt. Spending only a few minutes crafting her fly, she quickly rushed out on the dock by the flowing water of Upper Dam Pool.

Within a few casts, she hooked onto a spirited brook trout. After a long and laborious battle, she managed to net the fish and quickly took it to the closest resort to be weighed. Much to everyone's surprise, Carrie's fish weighed 6 pounds, 13 ounces, was 23 3/4" long and 15" around.

At the urging of some friends, Carrie entered the fish in the 1924 *Field and Stream Magazine* Fishing Competition. She took second place for her trophy, and when the publishers told readers that she had caught the leviathan on a fly that she had created, the mail poured into the tiny western Maine Post Office with orders for her fly. She was soon in the commercial fly-tying business, eventually creating a pattern that was sold worldwide. Today, Carrie's Gray Ghost is a popular casting fly, but is better known as a smelt-imitating trolling streamer.

Several other Maine anglers have created trolling streamer patterns that have become etched in anglings' annals and are still in use today. Dr. Hubert Sanborn of Waterville created a black and green streamer in 1936 with a unique method of mounting the wings. Instead of tying the saddle hackles along the edge of the hook, he tied the green saddles flat on the top edge of the hook. The first time he trolled this fly while on Messalonskee Lake, he caught a nine-pound, three-ounce salmon, naming the fly the "Nine-Three."

Sebago Lake, where the landlocked salmon was first classified, is also the home to a famous angler and a famous trolling fly. Legendary guide Art Libby of Standish had probably spent more hours than anyone fishing Sebago Lake. In 1972, he experimented with an odd-looking fly that was tied as sparsely as it could be and still be recognized as a piece of fishing equipment. His fly, the Miss Sharon, named for his daughter, was an instant success on the big lake. Libby tied four layers consisting of white, orange, red and black bucktail to a #4 hook that was wrapped with silver flat embossed tinsel. Under the tinsel was a connector of 50-pound monofilament with a #10 treble hook on the end. Libby specified that the fly be tied full in the early spring and then sparser as the water cleared.

Several other patterns remain at the top of the trolling angler's list and are dragged for countless miles through Maine's cold-water lakes. The Umbagog Smelt, named for the popular border lake captures the smelt's purple breeding hue and accounts for many of my early season salmon, as does the Flashy Joe's smelt pattern. Likewise, many anglers use a variation of Carrie Stevens's "Ghost" pattern with flies like the Green Ghost or Red Ghost having staunch supporters for one reason or another.

The Gear

The mechanics and equipment behind traditional fly trolling vary from angler to angler, but many commonalities exist. To begin with, most anglers use a stout fly rod, preferably nine feet or more in length. Aside from providing a more enjoyable fight, the long fly rod serves to get the angler's line away from the boat. When trolling on fabled Sebago Lake (home of the world's record 22-pound, 8-ounce landlocked salmon taken in 1907), I often motor past Frye's Leap in Raymond where the water is extremely deep and my rod tip actually touches the granite cliffs. I use a nine-foot 12-weight saltwater fly rod that features a large fighting butt and double handgrip.

Frye's Leap on Sebago Lake rises out of the water and is a popular spot for fishing and even cliff-jumping for the daring.

For reels, almost any fly reel will work, but I prefer a multiplier-type reel that will bring in my line as quickly as possible. This is especially important when I am alone and trolling two rods. If I get a fish on one rod, I want to be able to bring the second one in as fast as possible to avoid a snag or tangle. I also appreciate the quick retrieve when I want to change flies. I use a Martin MG-72 reel, which has a 3-to-1 retrieve rate (the spool turns three times each time I turn the handle one crank) and an adjustable disc drag that can slow even the largest fish. You used to be able to pick these reels up used for under $25, but now they fetch upward of $100.

Rene Lavoie holds up a nice, plump salmon taken while trolling at ice-out.

When trolling a streamer fly, the fly line serves two purposes. First, it gets the fly down below the surface. The depth you reach depends on your speed and the weight of the line. Second, the fly line follows the course of your boat, unlike monofilament line that only tracks a straight course when you turn. The fly line adheres to the water because of the surface tension created by the large diameter line and follows the boat. If you make a sweeping turn around a dock or other obstacle, the fly line will follow that arc. Most anglers use an inexpensive eight-weight sinking level line.

Cortland has designed a fly line just for trollers that sinks at a rapid rate and is extra-long to allow anglers to get their streamers out to almost any depth. Their 333 Trolling Fly Line is 50 yards long, is level and comes in eight-weight. I had just started using this line on my reels and I was fishing with Bob Tiner and Rene Lavoie on Thompson Lake. I was catching fish like crazy and they had a slow day. Turns out my specially-designed trolling line was longer and heavier than their sinking fly lines, and I was getting my offering where the fish were. Guess who went out and bought the "new" trolling lines?

While the mention of trolling conjures up thoughts of boredom to some, most trolling anglers don't sit and let the fish come to them—they try to impart motion to their flies to entice finicky fish. When trolling bait, the rod is clamped into a rod holder while the boat and the bait do all the work. When trolling flies, the angler imparts action to the fly by pumping the rod back and forth to create the illusion that the fly is swimming. Most often, the fish will strike as the fly is motionless between "jigs". That fish may have been following the fly for a short distance and that pause was just the opportunity the hungry salmon had been waiting for.

Some ingenious anglers have developed a machine that will do the jigging for you. Most are made with a windshield wiper motor housed in a sturdy box and set up with a variable speed switch. Clamp your rod in the holder and flip the switch and your rod will pump back and forth, causing your fly to swim and pause through the water. I picked one up last year and use it primarily when I am alone, so I can work one rod and the machine can work the other.

Last spring on Rangeley Lake my jig machine caught fish when my fishing partner did not. The proof is in the proverbial pudding.

Retired Police Chief Bob Tiner, also a Maine Guide, shows off a nice white perch he caught while fishing with the author one day.

I enjoy trolling flies over other methods of trolling because you are always moving, trying to make the fly "swim". To many, it's a less boring method of trolling, and those new to the sport seem to like the action as well. When two anglers are in the boat, it is wise for each angler to try a different fly pattern and frequency of jigging to see what the fish want that day. On almost every body of water we fish, Rene will start off with a Barnes Special. This streamer represents a yellow perch, a species common in just about every Maine lake and was originated by Cecil Barnes, a guide from East Sebago. Sometimes merely increasing or reducing the boat speed is also enough to put the fish on the bite.

Trolling flies for salmon and trout in Maine is a tradition-steeped, time-honored method of angling that is still popular today. While some fly-fishing purists believe that only casting constitutes fly-fishing, many of our sport's forefathers would object. Trolling involves skill, requires the angler to be able to read the water and know where the fish are, and also be as well versed on matching streamer patterns to food sources as the wet or dry fly angler must be. With pioneers like Carrie Stevens and Art Libby as trolling advocates, you're in good company, fellow anglers.

Bait Trolling

Right at ice-out, I typically start with the same trolling setup, but I use live smelt on a sliding bait harness. Some old-timers still sew their smelt on, but I find the ability to quickly adjust the sliding rig so my bait slowly turns over in what Rene calls "the death roll" is much faster than re-sewing the bait when it doesn't ride just so.

When trolling smelt, you want to go as slow as possible. Most modern four-stroke motors will idle down to nothing, but many anglers opt for an electric trolling motor or will use a trolling plate on their outboard. I recently went high tech and bought a trolling motor that communicates with my fish finder so that the motor will follow a specific contour line. This system allows me to precisely follow the shoreline and stay in one exact depth. I joke that I could cook breakfast in the boat while the motor charts and follows the course.

For Rene and me, April fishing is about following the waters from south to north as the ice leaves from southern Maine up to the western mountains. We can typically get on Sebago Lake at the start of April. A few years ago, I was on the lake on March 17th!

Trolling the mouth of the Songo River puts anglers in THE hotspot for ice-out angling on Sebago. The smelt that run up and down the Songo at night congregate near the deeper water at the end of the navigational buoys and draw in hungry salmon and togue.

April

The sliding bait harness rig allows anglers to slow-troll smelt and adjust the perfect roll.

Anglers navigate out past the buoys to fish for ice-out salmon at the mouth of the Songo River on Sebago Lake.

From Sebago, Thompson Lake in Oxford is the next to see ice-out. For the last few years, Thompson Lake has been on fire at ice-out, with some decent, football-shaped salmon.

Next up on the ice-out agenda is Lake Auburn. Living in Auburn for more than 30 years has me knowing this gem like the back of my hand.

Finally, we end our ice-out angling with my favorite trip of the year—Rangeley Lake. Some years the ice is out before the end of April; other years we need to make plans in early May. It all depends on how severe a winter we had. I always make sure to leave my work calendar open from the last week in April through the first week in May. Priorities. The chance to catch a salmon up to eight pounds, numerous brook trout and unparalleled scenery make Rangeley my trolling Mecca.

Rangeley Lake Ice-Out

Back in 2001, my dad accompanied me on our annual ice-out trip to Rangeley. The camp was full, so Dad and I grabbed a room at the Town and Lake Motel. This put us right where we wanted to be—City Cove and Greenvale Cove. Rangeley is a funny lake, being nestled in the western mountains. The old adage that if you don't like the weather, just wait a minute, rings true up here. You may start the morning dressed like you are going snowmobiling, and end the day in a light shirt. Similarly, you may motor out at daybreak to slack wind, only to be blown off the lake by 10:00 a.m.

This trip was no exception. It was 28 degrees when we shoved the boat away from the dock and let our lines out. Using dead smelt, we caught a few nice salmon and an occasional brookie. Dad was no stranger to the water, but he was safety conscious, so I figured he would want to go in when the wind started whipping down the lake, battling our 14-foot deep-vee boat.

As the wind got strong, we couldn't troll slow enough to use bait, so I decided to switch to flies. Did you ever try to tie on a streamer fly while manning the tiller of a boat in heavy winds? It's fun. I put on a Barnes Special and tied on a Gray Ghost for him. We motored toward City Cove, hoping to get out of the wind a bit, but each time we made a downwind run, we caught a fish, so much to my surprise, Dad suggested we turn and make another run up the lake. We kept catching fish, but I knew we needed to get inside City Cove. I motored into the back of the cove and as I

April

Jerry Roth with a beautiful Rangeley Lake brook trout taken while trolling at ice-out on a memorable father and son trip.

swung out to make a turn, I could see Dad battling a fish. I brought my line in and could tell by the way he was handling the rod that he had a whopper on!

We were in shallow water, so I assumed he had a brook trout and the rhythmic thumping of his rod tip all but confirmed my prediction. He took in some line, but the fish darted sideways in the shallows and took more for himself. I tried to keep Dad facing toward the fish, making sure to keep the line away from the motor. No easy task in that wind. Finally, the fish tired and my dad got it

April

alongside the boat. I netted the leviathan. What a beautiful square-tail!

We had time for a quick photo and I measured the fish at just over 23 inches. I estimate it was at least four pounds, and close to five. The photo doesn't do justice to the thickness the fish displayed as I measured it. Dad and I talked about that trip, and the brookie, for years to come, and I can safely say that was one of our best trips.

While there are other lakes in this great state, these are the ones we know and fish. I've often wanted to fish the fabled waters of East Grand Lake, but it's just too far of a ride. On many mornings, I will fish a few hours before work, so driving to Washington County and back is out of the question.

Once the smelt stop running, the salmon fishing slows down as the waters warm. It's time to switch gears and troll for trout on some of the smaller waters in my region. Oh, it's also turkey season, so flip the page to May!

May

It's Trout and Turkey Time!

    An unusually warm May day got the better of me at work, so I left a bit early and headed home to grab my square-stern canoe. Powered by a vintage 3-horsepower Evinrude Lightwin motor, it's just the right boat for smaller trout ponds. I decided to fish Casco's Coffee Pond for its abundant and fast-growing splake, a non-reproducing hybrid between a brook trout and a lake trout. Coffee Pond has a very shallow launch that can't accommodate larger boats, so my canoe is just the ticket. Besides, I like the feeling of fishing from a canoe with the sound and smell of an old two-stroke motor. It surely brings back vivid memories of my angling youth.
    After launching, I motored for the western shore and got my trolling fly rod ready. When targeting trout, I like small lures like the Al's Goldfish or a small Mooselook Wobbler in an orange or hot pink color, but I had some frozen smelts left over from salmon trolling, so dead smelts it was (you can't use live bait on Coffee Pond).
    I stripped out about 75 feet of line and clamped the first rod on the port side and fiddled with my other rod to get it ready. I was trolling in about 15 feet of water when my rod began to

scream. Surmising I had snagged a rock or submerged log, I pulled the rod out of the holder and tugged on it. Nothing moved, so I was right—I had caught bottom.

As I shut off the motor, the bottom pulled back! I set the hook and again it felt solid, like bottom, but a few tugs told me I had a decent fish on the line. Excited by the apparent size of the fish, I played it gently, not wanting to lose it. I'd take some line in and the fish would take it all back, and then some. This went on for a few minutes; then the thumping started. The fish fought like a brookie, so I knew I had a splake. Finally, I got it close to the canoe and I was able to net the fish with my almost-too-small trout net. A gorgeous splake, quickly released to give someone else a similar thrill. This is May trout trolling in the state of Maine!

Trolling for trout in early May utilizes the same gear as we use for ice-out salmon fishing. The flies remain the same, but I find a few different lure patterns work best. Small spoons in the 2-inch or smaller size work well for trout, as they generally have smaller mouths than salmon or lakers. One of my favorite lures is the Al's Goldfish in gold or orange. These little spoons have some great action at trolling speeds of about 1½ or 2 miles per hour. I always watch the lure boatside and adjust the throttle, so I can see how the lure is running.

First patented in 1946, the Thomas Buoyant lure comes in myriad patterns and sizes. I prefer the $1/6^{th}$-ounce model in the brook trout pattern. Mooselook Wobblers, in the scaled-down junior size, do well on trout. I prefer an orange lure when targeting brown trout. Gold and multi-colored versions work well for brook trout and rainbows.

May of 2014 was a tough time for this outdoorsman. My mom passed away and with that, my dad lost his wife of 61 years. I spent a few weeks with him in Raymond after her passing, and we did the only thing that we could think of to pass the time—we went fishing. This time was crucial to both of us, as we hadn't spent time together like this in ages, since much of his day had been spent caring for her for the past several years. I decided to get Dad out of the house and hit one of our favorite May trout spots: Little Sebago Lake.

The author shows off a small brown trout, taken while trolling flies in May.

We launched the boat and motored to the eastern shore and got the rods ready. I used a Barnes Special and I set Dad up with Gray Ghost.

We trolled the shoreline in water ranging in depth from 6 to 20 feet, as Little Sebago has a rapidly changing bottom structure. We turned into one of the many coves, and Dad soon had a fish on. A sleek brown trout about 15 inches was netted, then released. Another strike turned out to be a large yellow perch, followed by a small bass. Finally, we got back into the trout and caught and released several more decent brownies.

The wind started to whip up, so I told him we would make one more trip through the most productive cove. He had another fish on and played it rather quickly. I put the net in the water and the fish saw it and darted deep. I lunged at the fish and the net slipped out of my hands and glided to the bottom. I was mad at myself as I really liked that net. Not to mention it wasn't cheap. With the chop on the water, I couldn't see it, so we motored for the launch and called it a good day. Despite losing my net, it was good to see my dad enjoying himself.

We decided to fish the next day, and it was calm on the water. I headed straight over to where I lost the net, and wouldn't you believe it, there it was in about 8 feet of water. It was easy to use a jig with a treble hook to snag it, and I retrieved my favorite net. We fished for a few hours and while we didn't slay them like the day before, we had fun. That was the last time Dad would fish in the boat with me, and it sure sticks in my head as a memorable couple of days on the water.

The author with his biggest brown trout to date; a 6.14-pound fish taken in 1995 while trolling a Gray Ghost streamer on Long Lake in Harrison.

West Carry Pond Antics

Many Mays ago, Rene and I made a trip up to West Carry Pond to fish for brook trout and togue. At the time you could use bait for fish on West Carry, and bottom fishing for togue was hot in May. Additionally, there was excellent brook trout fishing to be had.

May

Rene told me we had a place to stay, as his old fishing partner, Dick Parker, had allowed us to use his camp. Dick was aged and didn't get up to camp much but Rene had been there before, so he knew the camp somewhat. Rene told me that Dick admittedly had quite a mouse problem at the camp but had addressed that issue.

We got up to camp and got the boat in the water and moved our gear into the old-fashioned but comfortable lakefront abode. I went to the bedroom and unrolled my sleeping bag on one of the old spindle beds, but soon discovered the bedspread was covered in mouse poop. I've slept in some pretty bad places, so a few mouse turds wouldn't bother me at all.

It was suppertime, and my mom had made us a nice casserole. I turned on the gas oven, and a sour burning smell came wafting out of the top of the built-in stove. I looked into the burner and saw that a petrified mouse carcass was roasting from the oven heat. Maybe it was the bed-shitter. I told Rene and removed him with a set of kitchen tongs.

Once the casserole was done, I grabbed an oven mitt hanging by the stove to remove our dinner. I shoved my hand down into the mitt, and soon discovered where more mice had gone to die. We had several other mouse sightings during our brief stay at camp, and Rene dryly commented, "I guess Dick didn't do too well with his mouse-proofing." No kidding!

The following day we motored out and anchored to bottom fish for lake trout. I told Rene I had a treat for him, but didn't let on what it was. We each sent two lines out with slip-sinker rigs and were soon into the lakers. Nothing remarkable, but they were fun to catch.

I grabbed my knapsack and pulled out a few items I had not had in a boat before: a small gas stove, a coffee kettle and a medium-sized pot. I set the stove on the boat seat between us and started it up. In no time we had piping hot coffee. Then I got the pot boiling with a few inches of lake water and set a finned aluminum disk in the bottom. This was called a Bakepacker and it allowed you to bake items in a plastic bag using boiling water. Into that I plopped a bag prepared with cornbread mix. Mouse just shook his head and muttered, "Friggin' Tow-head!"

The author with a nice lake trout taken with a slip-sinker rig.

After about 20 minutes, I had one big piece of moist, steaming cornbread. A few pats of butter and some homemade strawberry jam rounded out the meal, and we enjoyed the best meal I ever had in a fishing boat.

The wind soon whipped up and we took to trolling. I put on a small gold spoon and let my line out, curling up on the boat seat to buffet the wind. In no time the sun, rocking boat and my full stomach put me to sleep. I woke abruptly when Rene told me I had a fish on. I reeled in and released a nice brook trout. I talked about that brook trout all day. Rene wasn't impressed, and chided me that had he not awoken me from the clutches of Morpheus, I would have missed that fish. For the record, he didn't say it that politely.

Each spring, during one of many fishing outings, Rene will repeat the old saying "Trout fishing is best when the leaf on an alder is the size of a mouse's ear." I don't check the alders, but I do like to fly-fish for trout at least once during the month of May.

The Cold Hurts

One brutally cold May day, Rene and I were trolling Aziscohos Lake in remote Oxford County. This man-made lake, created by damming up part of the Magalloway River in 1911, created a phenomenal salmon and brook trout fishery. Rene and I drove up for the day, packed a lunch and a thermos of coffee and tea. We knew it would be cold on the water that day, with strong winds and a possibility of rain. Spring comes late to the western mountains of Maine.

We had a good morning trolling dead smelt, and switched to flies when the wind picked up. We stopped for lunch at one of the picnic tables shore-side and enjoyed the warmth of the sun, but not for long. With the winds came a cold, sideways rain, but the fishing was still going strong. We didn't see any other boats on the water on this dismal weekday, and I was surprised when a small aluminum boat motored over toward us.

The passenger in the front was hollering something at us, but between the wind, rain and boat motor, we couldn't make it out. The two anglers pulled alongside us, and I could see they weren't dressed for spring angling as we were. Aside from being cold and wet, the fellow in the front of the boat had a bigger problem. He had a 3-inch Rapala floating minnow lure with a good-sized treble hook embedded in the meat of his palm, just below his thumb. He asked if we had a pair of pliers, which I quickly handed to him. He started to pull at the hook and I winced. Most any angler knows the best way to remove a hook, and if you fish long enough, you learned it the hard way—from practice.

Instead of at least cutting off the hook and pulling the barb through, he was pulling the hook out backwards. The blood was running down his arm into his boat. After a few seconds, he reefed on the pliers and ripped the hook from his palm. It hurt me just to watch and Rene remarked, as they motored away, that the cold was surely adding to the unfortunate angler's pain. Although, again, his words were not that gentle.

Playing Hooky for Trout

It was close to quitting time after a slow day at work a few years ago when I went on the road for a ride around the outskirts of Westbrook. I spotted the stocking truck at Mill Brook. It seems the folks from DIF&W were making their third drop of trout for the season. Now I typically don't follow stocking trucks around, but I must admit, I was excited. It had been years since I fished a small brook and it was a perfect, warm May day. I'd rather be on a remote trout pond trying for native fish, but this would have to suffice.

Feeling like a giddy school kid skipping class, I left work early and gathered the necessary implements. In less than an hour I was on the brook with fly rod in hand. I texted a few friends about the stocking truck—Matt Brunner and Josh Walton, avid fly fishermen in their own right—and they decided to join in the fun.

Now catching just-stocked fish is no easy feat. Not only are they adjusting to the shock of the transport and transplant, they are used to eating pellet food, not natural bait. With this in mind, my plan was to replicate an insect that may have inadvertently fallen into the rearing pond. Trying a few fly imitations and mosquito replicas proved fruitless. Then my fly box flipped to ant patterns. After I noticed a few trout holding against a log, my short cast found the right current and a 10-inch brownie was on! Keeping the fish away from a winter's worth of branches and snags was a challenge, especially on a fine 1-pound tippet, but before long a perfect brown trout sat in my creel. Another repeat performance and I soon had the makings for some smoked trout—one of my favorite spring traditions.

May

Turkey Hunting

The "invasion" of the wild turkey in Maine and the resulting hunting frenzy came slowly to this hunter, but suddenly they were here! I recall reading in the early 1990s that they were being stocked in York County, but because I didn't hunt down there at all, I half-ignored this news. Soon, we had them in my neck of the woods, but you had to be drawn for a permit. Before long, in 1996, I was drawn and I hunted and harvested my first bird. Next, the permit system was gone and you could hunt them spring and fall.

My first bird was taken at Frank Bowie's dairy farm in Durham. Frank was a family friend and had a good assortment of turkeys roaming his fields and woods. He had been sighting birds for years and once I had secured permission, I was there on opening day. With the help of a friend, I had set up where the birds had been dropping down off their roosts each morning. After hearing a raucous chorus of gobbles all morning long, the sun rose and "my" flock of turkeys left the security of their pine roosts and descended on the field about 75 yards in front of my hen decoy.

My pulse raced, as it appeared the birds were coming my way. I clucked seductively on my box call and waited. The birds didn't miss a stride and kept feeding and walking. Slowly, the lone gobbler in the flock took his group of hens to feed in the green field grass just out of shotgun range. It seemed like an eternity, but it was probably over in less than 15 minutes. The birds wandered over a small hill and were gone.

My friend and I were dismayed. Had I called too much? Did they see us despite our best attempts at camouflaging our bodies? Whatever the case, I opted to sit tight and wait. Perhaps they would return. My hunting partner disagreed. He suggested that we sneak up the field to see where the birds had gone. We were on private property with no other hunters present, so I knew safety was not a concern, but I was not confident that we could put the sneak on a flock of wary turkeys. His persistence got the better of me and I agreed to join him on his stalk. No sooner had he cleared the top of the knoll than I saw him crouch and motion for me to come forward. I inched my way toward him and as I cleared the knoll, I saw a regal Tom turkey strutting in the next field, all by himself.

He was only about 50 yards away, with just a thin strip of woods separating us. His back was to us and his fan in full display, so I felt I could get a few paces closer to him. As I made it to the strip of woods, I found an opening and prepared to shoot. He closed his fan and let out a gobble. As his neck was in full extension, I sent a charge of shot his way. My aim was true, and he went down in a heap. I had scored on my first Maine gobbler!

The author with his first turkey.

After that adventure, I would swear by the importance of hunting near a dairy farm with a source of undigested corn as feed. Although it seems that farms are on a decline, there are still plenty that dot the landscape. While many of the farms have ceased operation, the fields still exist and are usually cut for hay to be sold.

A maintained field is a boon to the turkey hunter, as birds will spend hours combing the field for insects.

That first bird came quickly and lulled me into a false sense that hunting turkeys was easy. I accompanied a few hunters on their first hunts but didn't get too fired up about turkeys for a few years, but that would change…

Seeing a flock of turkeys in the field behind my house all winter long in 2009 was just too much of a temptation. I had not successfully hunted turkeys since that day in 1996, but seeing them on a daily basis and having them within walking distance spurred me into gear, pun intended. After a long winter, the spring season was upon us and I had made the necessary preparations.

First off, I secured landowner permission from the late Russ Hammond, the farmer who owned the land behind my house. This isn't required, but it's always recommended, and it was nice to meet a new neighbor. The farmer and his family had been in the area forever and, at the time, he was leasing his field out to a man who raised beef cattle. I was granted permission as long as I didn't hunt when the cows were brought in, usually later in May.

I worked a blind into a thorn bush that grew about 50 yards from the edge of the woods where the birds roosted. It was the perfect cover. Each morning I would get up with the sun and pattern the birds. They swooped off the roost just at daybreak and there were 18 in all, including one big Tom.

Opening day came and I traipsed out to my spot. Two other hunters were walking in the same direction, but when I explained to them I had both a blind and landowner permission, they appropriately moved on to another spot. I crawled into my blind and enjoyed a cup of coffee while waiting for sunrise. After what seemed an eternity, the chorus began. Gobbles pierced the darkness and it sounded as though they were right in front of me. These were answered with more gobbles farther in the distance. Next came the crashing of wings and I knew my flock was coming into the field. It was legal time, so I prepared my shotgun in anticipation of what I thought would be a quick season. Hens and

May

jakes littered the field in front of me and seemed to keep coming, one or two at a time.

Finally, I got a glimpse of the big boy. He landed to my right and seemed to ignore the rest of the flock. I had set out two decoys—a hen with a jake towering over her. I was sure this would enrage the patriarch of the flock and get him to come closer. It didn't work. He walked away from me, up and over a small hill. I had an easy shot on a jake but decided to try and call the bigger bird over. After a series of calls with no results, I watched as the flock meandered over the hill and out of sight. I was crestfallen. How could he have avoided me? The blind looked good, the dekes looked fine, but no luck. I packed up my gear and headed home.

My next opportunity to hunt came a few days later and I was out in my blind again. This time I set up a lone hen decoy, in hopes of luring the big gobbler in. Like clockwork, the morning chorus began again, followed by the fly-in. This time the big gobbler landed much farther away than the rest of the flock, so he clearly was not interested in being around my set-up. The flock slowly moved to my right and out of sight. Again dejected, I pondered my choices. I was leaving the next day on my annual ice-out fishing expedition at Rangeley Lake, so my options were few.

I decided to take a jake if one afforded a shot, to get the makings of a slow-cooker turkey stew. I took out my box call and made a run of loud clucks, followed by slow, single calls. After setting the call down to take a sip of coffee, I noticed movement to my right. I saw a group of turkey heads bobbing across the edge of the woods in my direction. Peering through my blind with binoculars, I could see it was a group of four jakes. They were shoulder to shoulder as they made their way toward me, possibly looking for the sound of the clucking. A few more seductive clucks got the group to trot directly toward my blind. They saw the hen and continued toward her where she sat, just 20 yards to my left.

May

The group slowed when just 50 yards out and two jakes dropped off and watched as the other two continued on. I poked the barrel of my ten-gauge shotgun out of the blind and switched to the small box call strapped underneath the barrel. It purred lightly as the birds walked in, closer and closer. It was if these birds were joined at the wing bone as their heads were only inches apart. They closed the gap to within 20 yards and I decided to shoot. I held a Superpack license, which allowed me two bearded birds, and these fellows were sporting four-inch beards. I put my bead directly between the heads of the two birds and fired. They both dropped instantly with hardly a wing beat. It dawned on me that I had scored a two-fer! Turkey season was over for this hunter and I was on my way to Rangeley Lake.

Two birds with one shot!

The following year my daughter, Emily, wanted to get in on the action. Both of my girls grew up seeing their dad hunt and trap, but they hadn't expressed any real interest, up until now.

May

Emily's Gobbler

The alarm rang early, and with a little bit of coaxing, my preteenaged daughter Emily was up and enjoying a chocolate chip muffin as I checked our gear. It was cold on the morning of the youth turkey hunt, so I gave her one of my camo jackets to cover her up and keep her warm. The thermos that usually held coffee was filled with hot chocolate and we headed out the back door and across the field.

Long walks seem longer in the dark and we were finally in my blind, situated on the farm behind my house where we had permission to hunt. This was the same blind I had doubled in last season, so our hopes were high. I had been watching the flock since the snow melted. One huge Tom led the group, along with at least five jakes and more than a dozen hens. I would be happy if Emily just got a shot at a jake, as the big boy was very elusive and stayed away from me all last season.

It was fun explaining to Emily, an eager pupil, what the plan was. We set out two hen decoys close to the blind to lull the birds into a false sense of security. The birds were used to the blind, as I had put it up several weeks prior. We would wait for the birds to come off roost and hopefully lure a jake in with the two hen dekes. We sipped hot chocolate and listened to the morning noises while waiting for the sun to rise.

Emily was startled when the gobbling began, but I was elated because there were three distinct birds surrounding our spot. After several minutes of gobbling by the Toms, the hens started dropping from nearby pine trees and assembled in the field just in front of us. Emily remained calm as we watched the birds enter the field and begin to feed. From the tree line, four jakes started walking up the slight hill toward the rest of the flock, located within easy gun range. Behind them came a whopper of a bird, most likely the big gobbler I had seen last year.

Emily held fast as the small flock of male turkeys made their way closer to the blind. I told her that she could shoot either one of the jakes, but she insisted she wanted to try for the gobbler. I was pleased with her restraint. Her father, a veteran turkey hunter, had caved in last year and took the jakes when the big bird wouldn't cooperate.

As the group of five birds got closer, the jakes encircled the gobbler and the five of them walked together as if they were one. I had Emily get into position and poke the barrel of the shotgun out of the blind. We watched the clump of birds for what seemed like an eternity.

I started a series of light clucks to try and get the jakes to head toward our decoys. Two jakes took the bait and peeled away from the clump. Unfortunately, they stayed joined at the hip, too. I told Emily she could shoot a jake if they split up, but she shook her head and said, "No." She still wanted the gobbler. He had been puffing himself out, spreading his huge fan and we could see his beard dragging along the ground. She was impressed with all of this and wanted him.

Finally, the other jakes moved toward the hens as they passed alongside our blind and fed up the field. The gobbler was alone and in range so I told Emily to aim and squeeze the trigger. She was sitting in front of me with my ten-gauge under her arm. I was directly behind her holding her shoulders with the gun against my chest to help her absorb the recoil. A heavy semi-automatic, the recoil wasn't much, but I didn't want it to punish her. She whispered "I can see it now," so I told her to squeeze the trigger, which she did. The bird dropped instantly, incapacitated by a clean head shot at 20 yards.

We raced out of the blind and Emily attempted to hoist the bird up by his wings. He was too heavy for her, weighing in later at 22 pounds sporting a ten-inch beard. After several hugs, high-fives and photos, Emily tagged her bird and we gathered our gear for the walk home. A hunter was born and a dad experienced one of the proudest moments in his life!

May

A smiling Emily Roth with her whopper gobbler.

Scent Training Your Retriever Begins Now

    The Labrador retriever is a remarkable dog capable of enduring cold water, tracking down crippled ducks in tall swale grass and crossing the choppiest of oceans after sea ducks. Through natural selection and breeding, they were made for the water, plain and simple. With a dense undercoat, webbed feet for swimming and a rudder-like tail, the Lab is a waterfowler's dream come true. To the bird hunter like myself who enjoys duck hunting as much as grouse and woodcock hunting, the Labrador retriever proved a challenge—to take the animal's natural hunting instincts and channel them towards upland bird hunting.

Scent training begins when the dog is a puppy, like this rambunctious golden retriever.

To get a dog like a retriever, or any breed for that matter, to track and flush game, you have to train them to search out, recognize and locate the scent of the game you are after. With the specific goal of turning my chocolate Lab, Luke, into a grouse dog, I focused on scent training as the logical way to begin.

With basics such as simple voice commands and retrieving on land and water out of the way, I quickly wrote to a national dog training supply company and ordered a bottle of grouse scent. As soon as I opened the flip-top cap, pup nearly knocked me over in an attempt to get a sniff. His instincts were already showing through.

I began by giving him daily whiffs of the avian aroma, accompanied by praises such as "Good boy" and "Find the bird." By the end of the week, Luke associated the smell of the grouse with something pleasant.

Next, I began the actual work by laying down scent trails, first through the grass and later through the woods. I applied a few drops of the scent to a stick and dragged it on a meandering course across the lawn. Upon reaching the end of my trail, I would apply a few drops to the ground and place a dog treat in the center of that spot. This positive reinforcement acted as Luke's reward for following the trail to its origin.

Once pup knew his job, I took my scent training techniques away from the lawn and into the same woods we would be hunting that fall. This gave my pupil a new set of obstacles such as rocks, puddles and stumps to work over and around. I tried to imitate the random trail of a running grouse as I made my scent trail along the forest floor. Sometimes I would start from an elevated stump and other times I would run a trail into a hollow log, each time trying to imitate the deceptive tricks of a mature partridge.

As soon as I felt he knew how to follow a scent trail, I placed a bird replica at the end of the trail. By applying scent to a canvas dummy and tying grouse wing and tail feathers to the device, a trainer can come as close to a real bird as possible. This device can also be used in fetching exercises by throwing it into brush and sending the dog in after it.

As the weeks passed and fall approached, Luke was becoming a master tracker, his nose working open and shut as he scanned the ground hoping to get more of that delightful aroma. At this point, he seemed confident in the woods, so I decided to let him experience the real odor and action of a flushing bird. I took the dog to a favorite spot of mine that I knew always held birds. After a short time on an old tote road, I heard that familiar sound as Luke's nose worked for scent. His tail suddenly beat wildly as he crouched lower to the ground to get closer to the odor that he had found. All at once, a bird exploded in front of him and made for the sky. He snapped up and looked back at me as if to say, "Now what do we do?" I lauded him with praise and reveled in his first flush like a parent would marvel at their child's first steps. Now it was time to take my partner on his first hunt to show him just how this scent training applies to real life.

Your first real hunts should be relaxing and enjoyable, but oftentimes they are not. Until he has hunted numerous times and with other dogs and hunters, you don't have a finished dog. This will come with time and the best way to teach him fast is by taking your dog hunting every time you go. Also, by training on a variety of scents and birds, you can ensure yourself of a versatile dog suited to any upland challenge.

A few days into the season that October, a friend called to inform me that he had located a spot that was full of flight birds and invited us on a hunt. Of course, I jumped at the opportunity to introduce Luke to the peculiar scent of the timberdoodle and, at the same time, bag a few birds myself. His dog, a well-seasoned black Lab, was no stranger to hunting grouse, pheasant and woodcock. I figured that he would be a good example for my fledgling bird dog to watch. Luke would have no part of that, he wanted in on the hunt and often took the lead.

My friend's dog quickly jumped three woodcock that were swiftly downed by our party of four hunters. Luke wasted no time. He watched the birds fall and plunged into the thick brush. In no time, he came out with his first timberdoodle. As soon as I took that one, I sent him in for the second. That newly learned odor was surely etched into the recesses of his brain.

Several weeks later we were hunting grouse along a dirt road. As Luke passed by a marshy spot, he came to an abrupt stop in the road, as if someone had hit him with a two-by-four. He jumped into the brush and within seconds, a woodcock flew up and away, leaving me staring on in shock. The smell of his first two woodcock was definitely part of his repertoire of odors and he wasted no time in locating the bird responsible for that familiar smell.

As with any sporting dog, a Lab's natural instinct to hunt using their powerful nose is overwhelmingly strong. Scientists claim that the dog's sense of smell is thousands of times greater than what ours will ever be. In any case, by following the steps I used with my Lab and getting your dog out where the birds live, you can make your retriever into a more versatile hunting dog—a definite advantage for fall's vast bird-hunting opportunities. Training using scents, hunting with experienced dogs and reading up on the techniques that other trainers use all go hand in hand toward producing a top-notch hunting dog and companion. While some may argue that the often clumsy Lab is all feet or all tail, I'll say he's all nose!

As the waters warm this month, bass fishing kicks into gear and really heats up in June. Tournament bass anglers begin patterning fish and exploring new waters, camps get their docks in and summer officially arrives, so hurry up and advance the calendar to June!

The author's Lab, Luke, with the fruits of his scent training success.

June

It's Summertime and the Bassing is Easy

I was recently going through some old photos and I found what I believe to be a picture of me holding the first fish I ever caught. Standing on the dock, I sported a heavy red and white-striped kapok life preserver around my neck and what looks like a sunfish or bluegill on the end of my line. My grandfather is looking on from the end of the dock with his favorite fly rod at his feet, a rod I now have and cherish. The only caption on the rear of the photo is "September 1967." Since both he and my parents are departed, I may never know if this is my first fish, but since I was only 20 months old at the time, it has to be.

While my first fish may have been a small panfish, I caught countless smallmouth bass from under many docks each June, and still do. Some were lunkers and others were runts, but there is still something satisfying about casting a line out from the dock and relaxing on a June day.

June

The author at 20 months with what is likely his first fish.

Regarding that old photo of me on the dock, I am certain my mother took it while my dad was out in the boat fishing. I'm willing to bet that Pa saw me watching my bobber impatiently and decided to cast a bass popper near the weed bed close to shore.

I have vivid memories of fishing at age four. Again, my mom would have to chaperone me, as Dad was usually out on the water. I can recall filling a collapsible creel with sunfish that he would fillet and fry up with his catch. Later, as I got older, I recall seeing a three-section bamboo pole where my dad kept his fishing gear. I asked him about it and he told me he used it when he was a kid to catch perch off the pier. He allowed me to use it, so down to the dock I went. Once screwed together, it must have been 12 feet long. There were no eyes for line and no seat for a reel. Just an eyelet at the tip. I tied on about six feet of monofilament line and a hook and sinker at the end. I baited the hook with a night crawler that I had caught a few nights prior (I had a thriving worm business as a kid). Lowering the pole like a fulcrum, I dipped the worm in the water. Within seconds the rod tip went down and started vibrating. I leveraged the heavy rod upward and out of the water popped a 12-inch smallmouth bass. I had a lot of fun with that old rod that summer, and it still hangs in the boathouse.

The Dock

In order to fish from the dock, the dock first has to be put in the water. Starting in May and running through June, professional dock companies and fly-by-night "dock jockeys" rush to get the docks in the water so the summer folks can enjoy the water. When my parents bought our place on Sebago, Dad asked me if I could build a dock. Of course, I accepted the challenge. How hard could it be? Just make a four-foot by ten-foot box and cover it with decking. Make it from pressure treated lumber so it would last. Use pre-manufactured dock hardware to link it together. Piece of cake. I had that thing assembled in one Saturday. Of course, putting it in the water was another matter.

It was precisely at this moment that the old-timers from the island showed up to supervise. One suggested floating it out into the water. The other said I could use my canoe to get it in place. After much discussion, we opted to float it out. That meant getting wet and, although it was June, Sebago was chilly. I threw on my trunks while the supervisors remained dry and shouted directions and encouragement from shore. After a lot of treading water, a few swear words and a trip inside to warm up, I managed to get the dock in place. I can still see Dad sitting on a lawn chair at the end of his new dock smoking a cigar and surveying the lake.

June

Jerry Roth with a typical "dock" bass from Sebago Lake.

Removing the dock is much easier, as all you have to do is unbolt it and float it in to shore. No need for precision, as nothing has to be mated together.

Going forward, I decided to enlist some help from the ranks of the police department. I rented wetsuits for myself and a buddy, and we got the dock in by May each year, so I could get in on the spring fishing. The only issue was I could never get the same helper to come back. Despite my promises of inviting them down for summer joy rides in the motorboat, no one wanted to dunk themselves in the icy Sebago waters. Sensing I was running out of friends, Dad hired a crew to take the dock in and out going forward. Remarkably, I still have the original dock, but I too farm the installation and removal out to professionals.

First Fish of Summer

Each June, my girls scramble down to the dock once it is in and arm themselves with fishing gear in an attempt to catch the first fish of the season. This annual rite officially kicks off the start of summer. The girls typically fight over a little yellow and white Snoopy rod and reel combo that they first used as toddlers. I don't know how it has survived all these years, but it still works. I make certain to have enough rods rigged up with bobbers and hooks and I buy my nightcrawlers nowadays.

Olivia shows off a lunker smallmouth caught with the old Snoopy pole off the family dock.

June

Last year it was Emily who was first on the leaderboard with an eight-inch smallie. I think the year before it was Olivia with a lunker smallmouth likely guarding a nest under the dock. We always release the fish to grow or guard their nests, but we sure do enjoy the sport, as simple as it may be. I couldn't count the number of kids who have fished off that dock, myself included.

A number of seasons past, when I lived in North Auburn close to Lake Auburn, I was trolling for salmon on the lake. I hooked up with a slab-sided smallie while trolling smelt alongside the Spring Road. It was ice-out, April 7, and I had just motored across the lake from the East Auburn boat launch. I played out my line with a live smelt attached to a trolling harness and visions of football-shaped salmon in my head. As I neared a small stream that trickles into the lake, a slight tap, followed by a bend in the rod and a scream in the reel signaled a fish was on. I anxiously grabbed the rod, set the hook home and reeled it in. After a few moments, I lipped the green bass and brought it into the boat to remove the hook. Although I was hoping for a lunker salmon, my first fish of the season brought back memories of my early fishing days with my father when a bass that size would make me as nervous and giddy as the youngster I was. I decided to weigh my prize and the scale confirmed my suspicions that I had landed a respectable 4-pound smallmouth, a worthy trophy for most bass anglers. After snapping the obligatory picture, I eased the bass back into the cold waters, hoping that some other angler could enjoy a battle with him this month.

Later that summer on a calm, mild June afternoon, I slipped my canoe into the lake and paddled over to where I had caught my spring bass. I brought along a lightweight spinning rod with a Mepp's spinner, a lure from my youth. I could see the sandy bottom as I was in about six feet of water and I was on the shoreline of the popular Taber's driving range and food stand.

As the warm weather approaches and the weekend hackers visit Taber's to drive a bucket of balls to points unknown, invariably dozens of balls end up in the lake. While paddling along the shoreline and looking for spawning beds, I came upon numerous beds with large, round, white objects inside them. If I hadn't known better, I would have blurted out that the bass on Lake Auburn sure lay some mighty big eggs! The errant golf balls looked just like scattered white chicken eggs in the spawning beds. Perhaps this year I will try my luck at fishing golf balls from Lake Auburn. If you see someone plucking objects off the bottom of the lake, exclaiming "There's another one," pay me no attention —it's been a slow day on the lake.

With spawning in full force, June is the top month for bass angling.

Dad and I enjoyed our bass fishing in June. We spent quite a bit of time together in the boat both at sunrise and then after supper as the sun set. When I was younger, Dad would run the boat and motor to one of his favorite spots and then row along the shoreline. Or later, when we got an electric trolling motor, he would use that to move parallel with the shore and stop to cast a section of shoreline. His tackle box was magical to a youngster, and huge. It held all kinds or lures, many old-fashioned even then. He had hooks and sinkers and a box of cotter pins for the old outboard. I will never forget the smell of that tackle box and I can easily go down into the basement and take a whiff down memory lane.

June

We did very well casting toward shore in June, as the bass were on their spawning beds. Dad used Mepps spinners a lot. I tried the newer spinnerbaits and also liked the rubber worms with the propeller in front. Some days were epic, with 20 or 30 fish an outing. Dad typically had his blue crusher fishing hat on or a baseball hat with his company logo. Most evenings he would enjoy a cigar while angling, another smell I vividly recall. As I got older, I was allowed to pilot the boat. That allowed Dad to try other techniques. Sometimes he'd throw a minnow or crayfish on a hook below a bobber and let it follow behind us. We caught a lot of fish with that method. Other times he would pull out the old wooden Jitterbug lure and skip it across the surface. He was ecstatic when a bass smashed that lure, as was I!

Bass angling remains excellent this month. But the lakes get busy as July approaches. The waters warm and fish go deep. Die-hard anglers target the behemoths of the bottom, the togue. Flip over to July and go deep, young man!

July

Deep Angling for Summer Togue

When hot July days and nights send the respectable angler in search of shade, our lake trout seek the cool comfort of deepwater pockets. Maine has some top spots that produce trophy togue, even in the dog days of summer.

Anglers seeking trophy togue can use two basic methods: trolling or still fishing. Trolling anglers fall into a variety of categories, but primarily, anglers either troll bait or they troll lures. Bait anglers have a simpler choice: shiners or smelt. Many will argue the natural food for togue is the rainbow smelt and opt to use fresh or frozen smelt. This time of year, it is hard to find live smelt, so frozen may be the only choice.

Plugging is a time-honored method for taking togue while still fishing with bait. Plugging consists of utilizing a slip sinker rig, also known as a fish-finder rig. Today, most anglers use an electronic fish-finder to locate a fish or group of fish on the bottom, and then anchor within casting distance. As soon as the bait settles to the bottom, anglers leave the bail open on their reel and secure it in a holder. By leaving the bail of the reel open, the baited line can flow freely through the open tube of the fish-finder rig as the bait swims seductively near the bottom of the lake.

July

The author with a decent lake trout he caught while fishing bait on bottom, or "plugging."

The fish-finder rig is an essential piece of tackle for bottom-fishing anglers on our area togue lakes, and they should bring along an ample supply. Togue are known to wrap tackle around submerged logs and rocks to avoid being caught. I've used this method successfully on my favorite togue waters: Sebago Lake, Thompson Lake and Lake Auburn but togue anglers on any water can use the same methods.

Many anglers use lead core line and add a lead rudder to really get the line down fast. Anglers attach the lead rudder to the lead-core line with stainless steel wire. I rig my trolling lines in the following manner: first, I attach the lead-core line to a heavy-duty brass barrel swivel. Next, I twist a two-foot section of .029 diameter 174-pound test steel wire to the other end of the swivel. The wire is then attached to the rear portion of the lead rudder. From there, I run four feet of 20-pound monofilament line to a bait harness, fly or lure. I opt to use 20-pound test when after togue, knowing Lake Auburn or Sebago Lake can produce a monster at any given moment. Interestingly, my lead rudders were crafted in

July

Auburn by H and J Tackle, a company started by legendary local angler, Clayton "Clayt" Hamilton, beginning in the early 1940s.

Other anglers prefer lead core line with a dodger or flasher followed by a leader with a fly, lure or baitfish. You really need the lead core line to get your offering down, but each angler has his or her own method after that. I like the dodger and fly method, preferring to use a Barnes Special or Gray Ghost on any of my togue outings. A bait harness with a frozen smelt or live shiner works well for many other sports. Sewn-on smelt are also popular by those die-hards who still practice this art.

Lures are another top way to troll up big togue. Mooselook Wobblers, DB Smelts and Helin's Flatfish work well when towed behind lead core line and just bumped along bottom. It takes a skilled angler to keep the lure on the bottom without snagging a submerged rock, but those who keep their bait down low reap the benefits of their skill and care. When I have clients and want them to work the rod, I'll set out a flatfish when we are over one of the sandy stretches like off Nason's Beach. Nothing beats the thrill of a big laker slamming a flatfish on lead core line.

Downriggers are very popular on Sebago Lake and not only help togue anglers, but summertime salmon anglers, too. Salmon find a certain temperature and hold in that depth. Locating fish with a depth finder and sending lure or bait to that precise depth is a sure-fire way to get a July catch.

There is quite a fraternity of summer anglers who fish the big lake almost every day. I knew these guys were running downriggers and I knew they were catching fish, so I decided to join the club. I wanted a downrigger that would adjust to the water depth and keep my lure or bait just off bottom—prime togue territory. I did my research and found out that Cannon makes just such the rig. I outfitted my fishing boat with two Digitroll 10 units which feature a built-in depth finder and allow the angler to specify how far off the bottom he wants the cannonball. After learning how they work and conducting a few shakedown cruises, I have to say I am impressed. These things catch fish! Now I'm up with the sun most summer mornings working the depths and catching lakers or taking clients out on weekends showing them just what a lake trout is like to catch and what a beautiful lake I live on.

The author guided sports Tonya and Kevin Fletcher to this nice Sebago Lake togue.

July

Jim Bell shows off a great lake trout taken while angling with the author.

I've found that copper lures work best, so I've been running copper Mooselook Wobblers or the Williams Bully lure in copper. Taxidermist Christian Carlson has done a great job reviving the old Sutton spoon and his Northeast Troller line of spoons some in a multitude of colors, including my favorite, copper and nickel. I've also tried the imitation rubber smelts like the Gulp product line. They seem to catch fish every bit as well as the real deal, and aside from frozen or pickled smelt, they are the closest thing to a live smelt. Plus, they are much more durable than frozen or pickled smelts.

Early morning outings on any Maine lake will typically help you avoid recreational boaters, especially on Sebago and Thompson Lakes. For this reason, I like to have my morning coffee on the lake as the sun comes up and then I'm off the lake as soon as the first jet-skiers hit the water. Usually I've netted a few togue, as well.

Dog License Blues

One summer, many years ago, I was a young cop with a young chocolate Lab. Luke was a handful and despite the fact that I wanted to breed him, my veterinarian suggested that I neuter him, to perhaps slow him down. (I underwent a similar procedure years later and it didn't seem to have that effect on me, but enough about that.) I had the deed done on Luke, and the dog looked at me with disgust for a few weeks.

I had neglected to renew Luke's dog license, so I headed into City Hall to accomplish the task. Esther Gammon was one of the clerks at City Hall and I knew her well as she used to work at the Police Department. She is a nice person and a good sport to deal with the crew we had. With checkbook in hand, I told Esther that I needed to renew Luke's dog license. She walked over to the counter and began the process. I asked her if the price went down if the dog had been neutered and she stated it was a substantial savings. I announced that Luke had recently undergone the unfortunate procedure and I would like the discount. Just as I planned, she told me that I would need to provide proof. Trying to contain my giddiness, I told her that I had it in my truck and would be right back.

Out I went to get Luke, who was in on the joke. He was a little uneasy about entering the building, but once he realized it was not the vet's office, his tail started wagging. I marched him into the clerk's office, picked him up and placed him on the counter and lifted his tail, proudly exclaiming. "Here's your proof, Esther!" Esther immediately replied, "Get that damned dog off the counter, you fool!" We completed the paperwork and off we went. I still laugh about that anytime I run into Esther.

July

The author's chocolate Lab, Luke, after his dreaded surgical procedure.

July seems to drag on as the days heat up. An afternoon dip to cool off followed by a nap under a humming ceiling fan is good medicine for these sweltering days. But wait, August promises more of the same, so head to the coast where it's a tad bit cooler.

August

Head to the Coast for Striper Action!

We started out bright and early on an August morning that promised to bring a sweltering day. Launching my boat into the fast water of the Kennebec River in Phippsburg put me in some prime striper waters. After a short motor upstream, I turned on the fish finder. "Something must be wrong with this thing," I remarked to my fishing partner. "It's showing fish all over the screen." We each affixed a 4-inch silver Rapala minnow to our lines and played them out into the current. I adjusted the motor so that it would just move us slowly forward against the strong push of the outgoing tide.

No sooner had we both gotten both lines out, when my friend had a fish on. I reeled in my line and jockeyed the motor so he could play his fish. This was his first time fishing for striped bass and he was intent on landing this fish no matter what. We had been after salmon and togue together but he hollered to me that this fish had to be huge as his rod was nearly doubled over. Apparently, my fish-finder was working just fine and we had hit a school of stripers returning to the sea with the tide.

August

First the fish dove, then it surfaced, next it pumped on his rod and then let up. Seconds seemed like an eternity for this novice saltwater angler, hoping to land what he thought was at least a 15-pound fish. The fish was finally tired enough that we could get it close to the boat. I grabbed the silvery striper and hoisted it out of the water for my friend to admire. At first, I thought he would be disappointed that the fish was not the leviathan that he surely was picturing in his mind. The look on his face, however, told a different story. Clearly, this was the birth of a striper fisherman, after landing one of the fightingest fish that Maine has to offer. "Let's troll past that spot again," my friend shouted as I motored downriver and hoped that I could get a bite this time. Striper fishing in Maine has taken off at a tremendous pace for obvious reasons. With increasing native stocks and a strong restoration program in place, Maine and its Kennebec River have earned national and worldwide acclaim for striped bass fishing. It is true that the fishing has slowed down over the past few years, but the stripers continue to invade our coastline and charge up our rivers.

While some anglers gear up and head out into the ocean after large trophy fish, many anglers have discovered the thrill that the smaller schools of stripers, affectionately called "schoolies," can provide. Knowing a few sure-fire tips on when and how to fish for them can almost guarantee that the angler can catch and release as many as 30 to 40 fish per day, when they are in. That's not a bad day on the river, in my book. All it takes is a boat, a few rods with much of the same tackle you'd use for freshwater species and you are in business.

Knowing when to fish for stripers is as important as knowing where to go. Most anglers fish the outgoing tide. Fish usually retreat to the ocean with the tide, conserving energy and feeding on the way down. When the tide flows out of the Kennebec River, the current can be extremely strong, so a 9- or 10-horsepower outboard is the smallest I would want to use. Sometimes I have to run mid-throttle just to stay in place when the tide drops. Fishing the top of the incoming tide and the slack period at high tide is also quite productive, as schools of stripers often follow the tide back in, as well.

Reading the river is also another important aspect of striper success. While schools of smaller fish are easy to spot on your electronic fish finder, larger stripers hang out where there is sufficient structure to protect them and offer them a place to hide and wait for a meal to float by. Spots such as underwater ridges and humps provide a striper with a break from the current on the downstream side. Deep holes and channels also provide a rest from the current.

For the angler without the luxury of a fish finder, the surface of the water often gives a clue as to what lies below. Watch for faster water in one spot, unusual surface patterns such as circular patterns or a boiling appearance on the water. These usually indicate irregular bottom structure that should be worked.

Once you've located a school of fish, stay with them. I've located a large school of stripers and caught fish each time I trolled by for almost 45 minutes. That was some furious angling! When I locate such a honey hole I usually take out my fly rod and cast for bass, hoping to experience the thrill that only a striper on a fly-rod can provide. For this reason, I always carry a fly-rod, rigged and ready to go at a moment's notice.

Fly-rodding for stripers is one of the hottest sports around, with guides and equipment manufacturers scrambling to meet the demanding market. New fly patterns are being created every day, and almost every fly-rodder that lives near the Kennebec River has been tempted by the lure of this feisty gamefish.

Casting toward structure is usually productive, but anglers used to working small sections of a stream or pond are often dismayed by the size of the river and the seemingly endless spots to work. For this reason, I usually troll with lures until I locate a school and then work a fly in that spot. It helps to have two anglers in the boat, one to run the motor and keep the boat above the spot you are fishing, and the other to fish. Taking turns is perhaps the most sportsmanlike way of deciding who fishes and who pilots the boat.

Oftentimes, while watching the water for structure, you will spot a portion of the river that appears to be boiling. This can be a submerged rock or other structure, but it can also indicate a school of stripers attacking baitfish. This is the ideal time to take out your fly-rod and start working the school. Start out by fishing just under the surface and then increase the depth your line sinks to until you find out where the fish are. When they feed near the surface and make the water boil, you can usually catch one just under the surface with almost any bait-imitating fly. Anglers regularly take trophy stripers from the Kennebec River, but most anglers catch the smaller schoolies.

While it would be great to catch a once-in-a-lifetime trophy, anglers who concentrate on the easy-to-catch schooling stripers seem to have just as much fun. With daily catches of 30 or more fish, rod-bending fights with spirited fish and memorable days spent on one of Maine's most productive rivers, angling for schoolie stripers is one sport that can't be beat!

Angler Chad Syphers shows off a nice "schoolie" striper he caught while fishing with the author.

Bear Season

Many Maine hunters and countless sports from away head to the woods in August for bear season. Many of us will hunt a lifetime and never get a glimpse of the ghost of the woods. Maine's bear population continues to climb and more frequently city-dwellers are finding nuisance bears in their garbage or bird feeders.

A do-it-yourself bear hunt is tough work, requiring regular visits to your bait site, proper scent control and a stealthy approach to your stand. Guided hunts offer a better chance, as the guide has patterned the bear, lugged in all the bait and will dress and drag your bear out of the woods. I've been on both types of hunts and have harvested two bears in my hunting career.

My first bear was on a guided hunt in New Brunswick, Canada. The Canadian government is good about bringing authors up to the provinces, so I went on a fantastic grouse, woodcock, goose and duck hunt with the late Earl Peterson. I wrote an article for the National Rifle Association's *American Hunter* magazine that booked the entire following season for Earl. He was gracious, so he invited me up for a hunt.

New Brunswick has spring bear hunts, and these bear are generally big and hungry. My first evening out we set up in a promising stand but left when woodcutters started working nearby. We moved to a new location and I was in the tree by 3:00 p.m. As the evening crept along, I was beginning to think there were no bear within a dozen miles when Earl whispered, "Big one."

Sure enough, a big black bear was walking toward the bait bucket. The bear was a whopper, and I wanted it. I had plans for a rug, and this would make a beautiful one. The ambling bruin paused on a dirt trail and I lined up the front shoulder and fired. Down it went. I could see the bear expire, so we walked up and claimed my prize, a 305-pound sow with no cubs. Bear hunting, I thought, was pretty easy.

The following evening, we went to another stand so I could get some pictures and video. We captured two bears sparring on their hind legs—quite a sight. But that was nothing compared to what transpired next.

Earl had a rifle "just in case," so I wasn't concerned around the bears until one decided to get up close and personal. Seems the wooden stand we were in looked like a jungle gym to the bear, so he decided to climb the steps. I was right at the top of the steps, and Earl was to my left. I glanced at Earl to make certain he had the rifle ready. He did. That damned bear climbed up until he could sniff at my boots. Any farther and he would have detected another smell. I half wanted to tap him on the snout with my boot, but decided against it. Once he felt he got enough of my boot leather, he turned and climbed back down. No chance for a photo, I was frozen. But what a photo that would have been!

The author with his first bear and his New Brunswick Guide, the late Earl Peterson.

I baited for several seasons in Maine with no luck. These were the days before game cameras, and the old trail-timer was all we had to monitor traffic at the bait site.

August

In 2000, I was lucky and drew a cow moose permit and a doe permit. One of our dispatchers, the late Tim Emmert leased bait sites from the State near Nahmakanta Lake and invited me up, so I could possibly get "the big three"—a bear, deer and moose. I jumped at the chance even before he told me the details. He had some pals he had made from New Jersey, one was a cop and the others owned a fabrication shop. Tim had been tending the baits and had several bruins coming in. He told me all I had to do was bring my gun and a tent to sleep in and I could use one of the producing stands. I wanted to be a good guest, so I inquired if they needed any food. He said they had that covered: lobster and clams one night and a full steamship round of beef the next made up the menu. I told Tim I would cover breakfast, so I packed my griddle for blueberry pancakes, maple syrup and thick-cut bacon. If we didn't get any bear, we were certainly going to eat like kings!

Bear tracks in the mud by your bait site is a good sign.

I arrived the day before my hunt and watched these guys from New Jersey unpack the strangest contraption. It looked like a steel cage with gears, a chain and a motor. Next, they pulled the ice chest out of the walk-in cooler. Oh, did I forget to mention the cooler? Tim had a full-sized walk-in cooler on a trailer being run by generator. What a rig! When they opened the ice chest, there was a 30-pound side of beef marinating in all sorts of yumminess. The steel contraption I described was a rotisserie to slow cook the meat next to an open fire. It took several hours but around 9:00 p.m. that evening we feasted on the most delicious steak I ever ate. Charred on the outside with hardwood flavor and tender on the inside. I can still taste that damned beef.

I slept like a baby with a full belly that night, underneath the stars of beautiful North Maine Woods. The following day I cooked a thank-you breakfast for my hosts and we lounged around the campsite until midday. Tim escorted me to my stand, a comfortable ladder stand at the base of a hardwood ridge. I climbed up to my seat and settled in. Tim said he could likely hear me shoot from camp, but if not, he'd be back after sunset.

I sat in the stand enjoying the peace and solitude of the big woods, still shaking my head over the level of campcraft that these guys had achieved. They made this trip for many years and developed some great friendships. This is what is so special about sharing Maine's natural treasures with other like-minded souls.

It didn't get dark until 8:00 p.m. so I expected to be waiting until then to see some activity. It was only 5:00 p.m. and I saw movement to my right by a thick stand of alders. Sure enough, a black blob emerged from the alders and was on a fast-paced walk to the bait bucket. The bear was not the whopper I shot in Canada, but I was going to tag anything but a cub. It headed right to the bait barrel and started eating the donuts and bread within. I took aim and fired just behind the front shoulder and the bear went over and rolled twice before expiring. I was one-third of the way to my quest.

Tim arrived quickly as I was just putting my tag in my bear's ear and we carted it off on his ATV and gutted it away from the bait. I tagged it in Kokadjo that evening and Tim kept it in his cooler, assuring me he would take care of it. I headed home and let the crew enjoy the rest of their hunt. When Tim got back, he called me to pick up my meat. He had the bear's shoulders smoked

August

into hams and they were incredible. We even took along some bear ham on the moose hunt later that fall.

Bear sign, such as a clump of hair on a branch, signifies a bear's presence.

Yes, I did take a cow moose that October and I shot a doe in November. None of these were big trophies, but the hunts were certainly memorable. Not all bear hunts are as easy or as luxurious as mine were, but anyone who puts the time in on their own, maintains a bait site and bags a bear should be proud—it isn't easy!

Summer winds down as school starts up and the summer folks go back home. I used to dread these events, but now I look forward to September and cool nights that last into the morning. Flip the calendar and come along!

September

Cool Salmon Waters Heat Up This Month

Ah September! Cool evenings and mild days harken back to late spring and early summer, but fall is just around the corner. While Maine deer hunters get their first crack at archery during the expanded season this month, die-hard salmon anglers—this one included—give it one last push before stowing their gear and pulling the boats for the season. Water temperatures drop and fish move around at varying depths, much to the delight of anglers. Monitoring temperatures and marking fish puts the savvy angler on the bite for salmon and togue this month.

In 2018, Sebago Lake anglers got a treat. Saint Joseph's College, in conjunction with the Portland Water District, placed a lake monitoring buoy in Lower Bay that provides up-to-the-minute feeds of water temperature, dissolved oxygen, chlorophyll (detects and measures algae) and water clarity. The best news is that anglers can access this data, too!

Because I spend so many days on the water in the summer, I was excited when news about the buoy was released. I quickly went to the App Store and downloaded the free app "Live Data Center" and selected "Sebago Lake" from the drop-down list. I was seeing the exact temperature at varying depths in real time.

One July day, I decided to put the data to the test. I saw that the water temperature between 32 and 40 feet was between 48 and 50 degrees, prime salmon temps. I set my downrigger in that range and let out some lead-core line for the same depth. Sure enough, I caught two salmon and a togue in short order. You have to convert meters to feet, but this was a great aid to anglers wanting to know at what depth the optimum temperatures exist.

The author slips a beautiful landlocked salmon back into the water so another angler can experience the thrill of the catch.

Inspect an old-timer's tackle box you find in a dusty basement or at a yard sale and odds are you will find a glass thermometer-like device. I remember they were called Depth-O-Plugs. You would lower this device to a set depth and water would rush in and when pulled to the surface, you had a few seconds to get a true reading of the water temperature at that precise depth. I was always told salmon prefer water in the 50- to 55-degree mark. Once you find that temperature, make note of the depth, and troll your offering at the same depth. Modern fish finders can do this much easier, and most of the better units have a thermocline feature to help find water temperatures and fish. Salmon are pretty

September

finicky about temperature, making them relatively easy to target this time of year, but the new-fangled buoy sure beats Grandpa's thermometer device!

Sebago sees a lot of boating and recreational action all summer long, but in September, the lake settles down and fewer folks race around in boats or on jet-skis. While I am always sad to see summer wane away, I relish the quiet of the lake as the season turns. Now my usual morning trolling sessions extend later in the day, and I often go out in the afternoon and fish until dark.

Sebago salmon devour smelts in the springtime, but unless you have frozen bait left over or buy pickled smelt, lures are the best bet this month. My friend Rene, a long-time Sebago fisherman, freezes up his saltwater smelt for trolling and always gives me an update of his stock as we get late into the season. This year I stocked up on pickled smelt, just to be sure to have enough on hand for this month. Other good options are the myriad artificial smelt imitations out there. I have run a few tests and found that area salmon and lakers bite almost as often on the life-like artificial baits as they do the real thing.

When you mark fish at specific depths or are attempting to present your bait or lure at a certain temperature zone, a downrigger is indispensable, so you will see many in use on the big lake by guides and recreational anglers alike. Whether you're targeting the bottom for togue or a specific depth for salmon, downriggers get the offering in the exact spot you want it.

Early this summer on Sebago, I trolled hardware behind my downrigger with success. Finding a thin lure that wouldn't dip below the cannonball was easy once I was contacted by a lure maker from Maine who has resurrected the famous Sutton spoons. Carlson's Northeast Troller puts out a line of heavy and light spoons in a variety of finishes. I prefer the thin spoons for downrigger trolling and found the copper/nickel finish drew in both salmon and lakers.

Other top September lures on Sebago include the Mooselook Wobblers in anything orange. Not sure what it is about that color, but Sebago salmon love it. DB Smelts, another thin trolling lure, work wonders on Sebago salmon this month, too.

Finding the fish is easy with a fish finder, even on a big lake like Sebago. Traditionally, fish hold in certain spots depending on the time of year. I find salmon and the occasional togue in shallower water this month, but they can be just about anywhere. With less lake traffic, trolling between Frye Island and Frye's Leap is easier. Fish seem to cruise this natural channel and it gets quite deep, even right against Frye's Leap.

I have an old 1960s map of the lake that has many of the old-time fishing spots named. One such spot is the Camel Pasture near Harmon's Cove where the bottom rises up sharply. If you can troll around the hump you will likely bump into suspended fish. These tactics will work on any lake with salmon and togue, but each lake seems to have a lure or fly pattern. Hard to figure.

The 2020 season was great on Sebago with September bringing some phenomenal catches. Alewives were super-abundant this year, showing up on the fish finder as big bait balls. We would watch for congregating birds; seagulls, loons and mergansers, and head to those spots to troll. The salmon were chasing the bait up to the surface and the birds were picking them off when they got too close to the top or were injured and floated up. All you had to do was troll through that mess of bait and you'd get a fish almost every time.

I was able to put my clients onto some nice salmon, but fellow guide Glen Gisel of Sebago Sport Fishing really delivered. He put one client onto a seven-pound salmon and another on an unheard of nine-pounder. It's fish like these that make me think perhaps Sebago is headed back to being the salmon hot-spot in the state. It's great to get some late-season fishing in, but don't forget to take advantage of the cooler days to give your hunting dog a tune-up before the fall.

September

Water Training for Dogs

With fall gunning season only a few short months away, now is the perfect time to hone your retriever's skills in the water. Whether you hunt Labradors, goldens, Chessies or any of the other breeds, a retriever that is not completely comfortable hunting lakes, ponds and marshes in a boat or canoe, isn't worth its weight in dog biscuits. By examining how and where you hunt, and including these scenarios in your training regimen, you should be rewarded with a well-rounded retriever.

The author worked his Lab, Luke, all summer long to ready him for upland and waterfowl season.

According to veterinarians, water training is the best form of exercise for dogs. Swimming not only provides a great cardiovascular workout for the dog, it reduces the chance of injuries such as torn ligaments or sprains, commonly associated with heavy, ground-pounding workouts on land.

Water also acts to cool dogs down, especially when training in these aptly-named "dog days of summer". Nothing is more relaxing on a hot day than a dip in the pond, and dogs know this too.

September

Even though the water training cools your dog down, it is crucial to not work your companion too hard on excessively hot days. Water can only cool a dog down so much and if pushed too hard, your pet may experience heat exhaustion. Signs to watch for are excessive panting, vomiting or diarrhea and/or a lack of energy.

For those of us who plan to hunt Fido from a boat or canoe, it is imperative that we train our dog to be comfortable when entering, exiting or riding along in such a craft. Many owners of top-notch field dogs are embarrassed when their seasoned pro won't get into a canoe for the first time. For safety's sake, no one wants an unsteady dog in a canoe or small boat when hunting on frigid fall waters. A slight weight shift by dog or owner could spell disaster for an otherwise enjoyable hunt. For these reasons, hunters utilizing watercraft need to make their dog feel at home in whatever they plan to hunt from.

When I started training my chocolate Lab, Luke, I demanded that he be steady in a canoe, as that is what I do most of my duck hunting from. I began by teaching him to sit still in the canoe while on land. I then gradually moved the canoe to the water's edge and had him make a series of short retrieves from the craft. From there, I paddled around in shallow water, while requiring him to sit motionless in the bow. Unfortunately, he was fascinated by the lily pads that floated by and would often lean over to snatch one out of the water. Whenever he did this, I would upset the canoe and put us both in the water. A few of those unexpected dunkings were enough to convince him to sit back and enjoy the ride.

Once he was comfortable as a passenger, it was time to teach him the proper way to enter and exit the canoe for a retrieve. I nestled the canoe in a shallow bed of reeds and tossed out a dummy. I then had Luke slip into the water from the raised canoe seat, so he didn't drag his hind legs on the gunwales, possibly tipping me over. Once he returned to the boat, I would take the dummy from him and grab his collar to assist him in getting his front paws inside. Once that was accomplished, I would push down on his neck to provide the necessary leverage for him to pull his hind legs in. I don't usually send my dog on a retrieve from the canoe, as we primarily hunt from blinds, but occasionally I will jump shoot on the way in to the blind, so learning the proper method to enter and exit a boat is a must.

Once you reach your destination with pup by your side, most waterfowl hunters utilize decoys, which can be a problem for some dogs. We've all seen at least one instance where a novice dog was sent out after a duck and returned with a deke—line, anchor and all. This embarrassment can be avoided by incorporating decoys into your water training sessions.

The best training scenario is the one that most closely replicates actual hunting conditions. If you set up a spread of well-spaced decoys, your dog can get the picture of what an actual hunt will be like. Begin by tossing the dummy out to the side of the decoys. A generous amount of praise should be given when the dog selects the dummy and ignores the bobbing duck look-alikes. Next, cast the dummy beyond the dekes so the dog must swim through them. Once he has mastered swimming through the spread, plop a dummy down in the middle of the dekes. An application of liquid duck scent to the dummy will help the dog home in on it as well as ignore the odorless objects around him. Just be certain not to handle the decoys if you have duck scent on your hands, or you will be sending mixed signals to your dog. When pup can make successful retrieves through, around and amongst the decoys, he should be ready for opening day.

While training and hunting a dog in water is generally considered to be beneficial for the dog, there are several health and safety concerns that cannot be overlooked.

First and foremost is water entry safety. We've all seen the photos of an eager Lab diving headlong off a dock or banking after a retrieve. While this may look impressive, teaching your dog to dive into unknown waters is a recipe for disaster. Each year, many dogs are injured when they collide with submerged rocks, pier supports and other hidden hazards. Just as you wouldn't leap off shore into unfamiliar waters, you shouldn't require your dog to either. Be certain to examine both hunting and training areas for such dangers.

A well-trained retriever adds a whole other dimension to waterfowl hunting.

Excessive water intake is also a problem with water dogs, especially those with smaller mouths. I used to toss tennis balls into the lake for my dog to fetch when I wasn't carrying a training dummy along. When we were finished, my Lab would sometimes drool or even vomit an amount of lake water. I discovered that the tennis ball did not fill his mouth enough for his gums to seal as they did with a canvas or rubber dummy, allowing water to rush in, which was apparently swallowed.

Ear infections are also a common malady when training a dog in water. Most of my training takes place in a swampy marsh, complete with thick lily pads, snags and brush that I am likely to encounter when actually hunting. The water here is very muddy and murky and as a result, my dog frequently gets yeast infections in his ears. As soon as I notice a brown, waxy buildup, or detect an odor, I massage a small amount of ear cleansing solution into Luke's ears with a cotton ball. A smile, a tail-wag, and a soothing growl are my rewards.

When you have your dog at the veterinarian for its annual check-up, inquire with them if there are any other precautions they recommend when training your dog in the water. By combining practical water training with your dog's natural instinct to retrieve, you can assure yourself that come hunting season, you and your friend will be ready for a lifetime of memories.

A Reflection on Opening Day

For hunters, the term "opening day" conjures up numerous images. Perhaps your thoughts turn to your first season afield. Or maybe you recall the preparation that went into your first day out in the woods. You might even have a story to share about the deer you bagged on the first day of the season. No matter how long you have been hunting or how old (or young) you are, opening day holds a mystique that only a hunter can know.

If you were to turn the clock back 40 years and could peer into the past, you would have the chance to witness the birth of a hunter. I don't mean that you would witness the moment when mother delivers child. Rather, you would see a teenager who was consumed with going after a variety of game, but who hadn't yet entered the woods with a rifle or shotgun. Beginning in the spring, our neophyte hunter spent several evenings sitting in a classroom of other wannabe's studying for his Hunter Safety exam. This was a relatively new requirement that was meant to increase the safety of the shooting sports. This young lad pored over the instruction manual, was quizzed by his father, and finally passed the test with flying colors.

Next came the gathering of equipment. An old pair of jeans would serve as hunting pants. Work boots did double duty as hunting boots and a hand-me-down orange vest and hat fulfilled the legal requirements. However, the most important piece of equipment was still in Grandpa's closet. Our young hero was fortunate enough to have a grandfather who was quite a bird hunter in his day and still hung on to his favorite fowling piece. Whether he planned to pass the gun on to a deserving grandson or he just didn't want to sell a part of his past, he still had the original Remington Wingmaster pump shotgun, chambered in the then-popular 16-gauge.

Several years prior, Grandpa had made a deal with this youngster that if he passed his hunter safety class and was deemed responsible enough to handle the gun, he could have it. When the time came, Grandpa lived up to his end of the bargain and delivered the shotgun to the boy.

Now all that stood in the way of a first hunt was the calendar. The few months before upland bird season opened provided enough time for the lad to practice shooting the gun and become familiar with it. Although the gun remained secure in a closet, Dad allowed the boy to handle it, work the action, practice checking the gun to see if it was loaded and clean the gun until the inside of the barrel had a mirror-like shine. Soon enough the calendar page turned to October and the opening day of pheasant season was the following morning.

Dad was a planner, so the equipment was laid out the night before. Boots, socks, pants, shirts, jackets—all were arranged so that they would be easy to put on in the wee hours of the morning. Mom got up with the men to make a pot of coffee and see the crew off to the woods. Dad suggested stopping for doughnuts on the way to avoid the delay of a lengthy breakfast. The son agreed, but would have agreed to anything to get to the hunting grounds faster. Dad had the stocking list from the state and had picked a spot that promised a healthy dose of pheasants and the possibility of less competition.

Turning into the field that served as a parking lot, Dad turned off the lights of the car and relaxed with a cup of hot coffee from the Thermos. His young companion grew restless, wanting the dawn to arrive. It finally did. When Dad declared it was light enough to safely hunt, the duo got out of the Oldsmobile and donned their gear. Shells were slipped into the elastic holder on the vests, boot laces were cinched in anticipation of a long hike and finally, guns were loaded. Although our young hunter had practiced loading and unloading the shotgun, the solid metallic noise it made when the first shell of his hunting career was chambered was unlike any sound he had ever heard and certainly one he would never forget.

The pair headed onto a dirt path that bisected a field of high grass. The cover looked "birdy" and the young hunter peered intently at any shape that vaguely resembled a pheasant's body. Once they were sufficiently away from the car, the father suggested that they start working the edges of the trail, hoping to flush a bird from alongside the edge. Despite his age, the younger hunter was tall, so stepping in and over brush, branches and downed trees was no problem. He worked the trailside like a bird dog, trying to cover as much ground as possible, remaining alert for a bird to flush. Dad had tried to describe the sound a pheasant makes when it takes to wing, but nothing prepared the boy for the sheer terror that a pheasant can create when it decides to leave its immediate surroundings.

As the pair came to the end of a trail where it met with another, things began to quiet down. Dad had left the woods and was standing on the path. Son had but a few more steps to take to get onto the same path. As soon as he put his foot down, just inches from the trail, the young hunter saw movement at his feet. It happened too quickly to frighten him. A hen pheasant leaped into the air, beating her wings frantically, trying to gain both distance and altitude. The bird began to level off as the young hunter shouldered the shotgun and took aim. Like a line drive, the bird gave the hunter a straight-on shot as it rocketed away. The hunter pushed the safety off and put his finger on the trigger. He slapped the trigger quickly and watched in awe as the bird crumpled in mid-air.

The prize was a small hen pheasant, but one look on the youngster's face would lead one to believe that it was a trophy elk or record-book white-tailed deer. Size, species or location didn't matter. A boy made his passage into the fold of a group known as hunters. It wasn't the kill that provided the excitement; it wasn't the meal that would ensue from game he harvested. It was the combination of all the planning that went into the hunt, the lessons practiced and learned, the tradition of handing down a gun to the next generation. All of these factors combined to make his first hunt one that he would vividly remember for the rest of his life. That young boy is now in his 50s with a family of his own. He has hunted a variety of game including caribou, deer, bear, moose, waterfowl, upland game and varmints. He has several trophies in his den that serve to remind him of hunts past. He gets nostalgic when October rolls around every year, even though decades have passed since his first hunt. As he pens these lines, he drifts back to that crisp fall day so many years ago, but his thoughts are soon interrupted. It is late September and he has decoys to repair, shotgun shells to buy and a rifle to sight in. After all, opening day is just around the corner.

The author, as a young man, with his first pheasant; a memorable hunt.

Salmon trollers eke out as many days as they can this month, before the boat is stored and the gear is put away. Archers have been stalking deer in the built-up portions of our cities and suburbs all month and have another month before the rifle crowd invades the woods. Dog owners get their pups in shape for upland season. Just when you thought summer was coming to a slow

September

close, October is on us with cover-busting birds and high-flying ducks. Flip the page! It's October!

October

Bird Dogs Don't Sleep This Month

The leaves have started to turn their crimson shades. Apple cider is once again a staple item available at farm stands and grocery stores. Pumpkins, gourds and hardy mums decorate houses as leaves blanket browning lawns. While all of these images signal that autumn is upon us, nothing spells fall to this writer like the opening of the upland hunting season.

For those of us who yearn to traipse along a dirt road or through the thickets with guns cradled in the crook of our arms, the ability to take a grouse, woodcock, pheasant or rabbit (along with other game) for the larder makes each trip afield a special one to be remembered for decades. All of these game animals are in season, providing the hunter with the ability to bring home a mixed bag for the makings of a game stew, but one quarry stands out among the rest.

To most hunters, the ruffed grouse is king of Maine's upland birds and is hunted hard from the first day of October, right up until deer season opens and shotgun is replaced by rifle. The ruffed grouse, or partridge as it is commonly called, has attained a well-deserved reputation as a tricky bird to shoot when on the wing, but it is equally as well known for its sheer stupidity when on the ground.

Hunters with dogs that can point and flush the bird probably have the best luck of all. The grouse will usually hold until the dog is looking it in the eyes before it flushes or darts off. If it flushes, a hunter in position has to hope the bird will choose a path unobstructed by limbs and branches. Typically, it does not. Sometimes it will hop onto a low-hanging branch and taunt the hunter to shoot it where it sits. Most dog hunters will forego such a shot for fear of striking their dog with a pellet. If the bird runs off, the well-trained dog will take up chase and can hopefully pin the bird down again. I have had a bird trot off a few yards away and not been able to locate it, so perhaps these birds do "run for the next county" as many suggest.

A well-trained dog makes it a joy to pursue ruffed grouse.

One of Luke's best retrieves came while Rene and I were hunting in Auburn. Now birds are scarce in that part of the state, so having a dog is a must. We were hunting a wooded spot that today is full of houses, but on that day, it was still just woods. A grouse exploded in front of Rene and he snapped his shotgun up and nailed it. The grouse locked wings and went down just ahead of us.

Luke went crazy and started working the ground where the bird flushed, making his way toward where it dropped. I expected him to prance out holding a dead grouse, chest puffed, but that never happened. I walked over to where the bird dropped and Luke was making tight circles all over the ground. We didn't see it fly off and Luke wasn't leaving that spot, so it had to be there. "Find the bird," I coached Luke, but I didn't need to—he was looking furiously.

Luke went by a downed log that was cut clean by a saw with the butt rotted out. He came back with his nose to the ground and drove his nose into the hollow log, coming out with a very-much alive grouse. What a find! There is no way we would have found that bird without the aid of a dog, and I still talk about that retrieve.

Most of us get our start hunting grouse by walking old logging roads in the morning hours when the birds begin to stir. Ruffed grouse spend their nights in the boughs of spruce and pine trees to shelter them from wind and predators. When the morning sun hits the dirt roads, they drop down out of the trees to warm up, feed on buds and insects and ingest sand that aids in the digestion of their food. These road birds will typically freeze when a hunter approaches, or they may simply step off the roads and sit motionless in the weeds and leaves. With their mottled brown appearance, it takes a sharp eye to spot a sitting partridge when the leaves are on the ground.

Road birds are also a prime target for "heater hunters"—hunters who ride the roads from the comfort of their trucks, stepping out to take a pot shot at a bird when one is spotted on the ground. While some may frown on this method of hunting, Maine's vast networks of logging roads make this a traditional form of hunting for partridge that produces results. While my favorite manner of hunting grouse is over a finely-tuned dog, I enjoy road hunting when going from cover to cover, knowing that I will get a chance

October

to stretch my legs when I reach my next destination, yet not willing to pass up a bird that is foolish enough to sit still for me!

Hunters who wish to hone their stalking skills for later in the month when deer season opens can do so with ruffed grouse. If you travel the back roads around your town, you can easily spot old homesteads along the side of the road. There may be an old cellar hole, or perhaps a pile of rocks that was once a fireplace. Once you find such a historical site, poke around a bit and you will likely find a patch of apple trees behind where the house previously stood. These abandoned trees often still produce fruit and draw grouse in to feast on the tart, tangy orbs that hang from the tree or drop to the earth. Once you know where an old apple orchard sits, creep in slowly and you may get a shot! I had an ancient, neglected orchard of several dozen trees at my old house that still produced apples, some 70 years after the trees were planted. I could see the gnarled trees from my kitchen window and regularly saw grouse pecking along the ground at apples and sapling buds.

To know what the birds are eating, inspect their crop. This grouse was into clover.

For stalk hunters, the end of the day also provides a window of opportunity to catch these otherwise wary birds off-guard.

Much like turkeys, grouse seem to sleep in the same tree, or at least one nearby, each night. If you are in the woods in the morning and bump one from its roost, you can probably find this bird and others close by when the sun sets.

Stalk Hunting

I went up to Bill Murphy's camp way above Rangeley at the start of bird season in 2019. We hunted the roads for most of the morning and I managed to bag one bird out of a covey of four. Bill suggested he drop me off on an old road that paralleled the main logging road and he would meet me where the two roads joined again in an hour. I liked the idea as I would rather walk than ride. Despite not having a dog, I figured I could put my stalking skills to use. This abandoned road was more grown-in than the road we were riding, but it was perfect bird cover. The staghorn sumac berries were ripe and dripping from the bushes while their vibrant red colors stood out in the drab forest. The first bird I shot had a crop full of them, so as I made my way along the road, I looked for clumps of sumac and scanned the ground carefully.

I hadn't gone more than 100 yards when I spied a bird on a stump next to a sumac bush. I aimed at his head and took him cleanly with the Ruger 20-gauge. Stalk hunting had paid off! After walking for about 15 minutes, I saw where a narrower trail went down toward what I guessed was a pond. It looked inviting, so I made a hard left down the trail. I could barely see along the sides of the trail, as the undergrowth was quite dense. At each opening, I crouched down and peered along the forest floor. I caught a bit of movement to my left and watched closely. I saw it again and noticed the head of a grouse bobbing as it walked just into the tree line. Like Sgt. Alvin York, I raised my weapon and waited for my quarry to betray its position. Out he popped from behind a tree and I took him. When I met up with Murph, I made the hand gesture for "2" and he nodded approvingly. "I put you in my honey hole; I knew you'd get something." Sure, this was a good

The author with a limit of four grouse, taken while hunting from Bill Murphy's camp above Rangeley.

road, but I think my stalking skills had something to do with my success, too!

Rene and I hunted with The Murph several times and what a bird year it was! Bill saw more than 400 birds that October and we limited out regularly. Most days we saw more than three dozen birds. Apparently, there were two, or even three, hatches that spring and hunters across the northern and western parts of the state had equally good luck. Yesirree, this was hunting like it used to be!

A few years ago, during deer season, I was sitting on the ground just inside the edge of the woods where field met forest. I was hoping to intercept a deer as it made its way to the field at dusk. Light was just beginning to fade when I heard a crunching sound. I readied myself, expecting to get a shot at a doe or buck in the next few seconds. The crunching got louder and I could not believe that I could not see the deer that was making this racket. Suddenly, I caught movement off to my left. A grouse was making his way across the carpet of dried leaves. When he was about ten yards from me, he flushed and landed in the spruce tree that I was leaning against. I looked up and could see him settling in for the night. Had I been bird hunting with a shotgun, he would have come home for a nice meal. But then again, had I had a shotgun with bird shot, the buck of a lifetime would have probably been the source of that noise!

Whether you opt to chase the king of Maine game birds with a pointing or flushing dog, walk the myriad paths that bisect the forest, hunt from the comfort of your truck or stalk-hunt these crafty birds, October is the best month to do so. With a backdrop of colorful shades of yellow, red, orange and brown, the days are milder and more conducive to a day-long hike along roads and trails.

Woodcock Challenge

My dad had two buddies that he liked to pheasant hunt with. They each had well-trained English pointers that were a joy to watch. I recall how excited they (the hunters) got when they stumbled onto woodcock. I didn't get the big fuss over such a small and livery-tasting bird. That was until I started to hunt them! These birds hold tight and are hard to hit, a wingshooter's dream!

The tiny woodcock holds tight for hunters and bird dogs.

In college, roommates Jeff Davis, Scott Wentzel and I hunted a series of three fields in Hudson, Maine, that had grown into alders with very wet ground. Woodcock love alder runs and moist ground so they can easily probe the ground with their prehensile beak for their favorite meal: earthworms. I took along my grandfather's old Lefever single-shot .410 and enjoyed the challenge of hitting a timberdoodle with this small gun.

I'll never forget the first time Luke and Turner each experienced their first woodcock. I was hunting Luke with Rene up in Eustis on a favorite bird run. We were on a dirt road and Luke was running up and down the road looking for birds. As if he fetched up on a solid lead, he jerked to a halt and stuck his nose into the grass at the edge of the road. A woodcock erupted from the grass and surprisingly I hit it. He forever loved the smell of that quarry.

Turner has an equally dramatic reaction to his first bird. I was fortunate to capture this moment on my GoPro camera and the scene appears in one of my YouTube hunting videos (see Troth1966 on YouTube). These diminutive denizens of alder runs and boggy areas are truly fun and challenging to hunt, so now I know what the fuss is all about.

The woodcock is fun to hunt using small-bore shotguns such as the .410, a 28- or a 20-gauge gun.

Pheasant Fun

We pulled over at the pheasant release site well before sunrise and got out to enjoy a cup of coffee. My hunting partner, Rene, was readying his gear as I was getting Turner out of the truck for what would be his first pheasant hunt. Another hunter walked over and noticed I had a different dog from years past as our dogs sniffed a get acquainted sniff. Well before sun-up, two anxious hunters jumped the gun and walked into the field. They couldn't see to safely shoot so we remarked that they would likely bump some of the birds, an upland *faux pas*. Once it was light enough to hunt, the other hunter suggested that he hunt one side of the hedgerow and we could have the other. That's how it should be done in our sporting world. We wished him luck and walked out to our claim.

Turner had been working with pheasant scent all spring and summer but hadn't been on live birds. I was optimistic as he displayed a keen nose, but this was the first golden retriever I had hunted. I kept him on a 30-foot check cord until I saw him working his nose to the ground, obviously locating bird scent. I gave him free rein and was pleased at how close he worked. Not bad for a one-year-old. He seemed a little unsure of himself and he watched me like a hawk, but he started to get birdy and stayed on task.

Once we got close to the tree line, he perked up and really began working the ground. His circle tightened and a hen pheasant erupted from the tall grass with Turner close on its tail feathers. I hollered at Rene but I didn't need to—he was on it, dropping the bird with one shot. Turner froze, watching the bird drop and, on my urging, went looking for the bird, which was obscured by the tall vegetation. The bird had some life in her, so when Turner got close, she took off on a run and Turner went ballistic, chasing and pouncing on her. He was unsure what to make of the feathery thing at his feet, but I knew right then a bird dog was born who would hopefully enjoy many seasons afield with me.

We hunted Turner two more times at pheasant release sites and he knew the game by this point. He even pointed on a pile of feathers left over from a predator kill. One trip up north for grouse got that scent pattern etched into his brain, too.

In 2019, without a dog to find birds, I decided to head out on the first pheasant release day and hunt anyway. I figured I could beat the bush, so to speak, and possibly scare a hen or rooster up to shoot. As I was waiting for daylight, a truck with New Jersey plates pulled in and a gentleman and his dog got out. We chatted about the hunting and pheasant release program and as the sun rose in the sky, my new friend invited me to join him and his dog. Elated, I of course accepted. Old Molly did a great job scouring the grown-up field for birds and put up three for us to shoot. Or miss! Hunters are a tight fraternity, but I will admit I was always reluctant to let someone shoot over my dogs if I didn't know them well. This guy sensed I was a sportsman and safe around dogs, and we enjoyed a nice morning hunt. Good times.

Rene and Turner with a successful flush and find.

October

In 2020 my good friend Adam Farrington had a young German shorthaired pointer named Rylee who was just a year old. He had been working her on the basics and she already had her natural ability rating from NAVHDA, the North American Versatile Hunting Dog Association. As he had done in the past, he offered me the chance to take her for a few days and put her on birds. A win-win for both hunter and dog! She had been grouse hunting once and did well flushing and finding downed birds, but grouse are skittish and don't always hold tight for a novice pup. I wanted to see how she did on pheasant as they typically sit until you literally step on them.

Rene and I headed to our usual release site and he was grinning, knowing she would soon be onto some birds. We waited for daylight and entered the field. I had Rylee on leash until we got into some tall grass. I let her go and immediately she drove her nose to the ground and began following a scent trail. I heard Rene holler "look at that," and saw a big cock pheasant running for the tree line with Rylee in hot pursuit! Sometimes these pen-raised birds get overfed and don't fly. That was the case with this fat rooster, or so I thought. He made it into the woods but Rylee was still right on his tailfeathers. All of a sudden he erupted from the trees and I missed him with both barrels, more stunned than ready for the shot. Rylee looked at me in disgust but got back to work. I ended up shooting my limit of two birds thanks to her solid points and it was a pleasure to introduce her to these fun birds.

Each year, biologists from the Maine Department of Inland Fisheries and Wildlife partner with local sportsmen's clubs and release pheasants in York and Cumberland counties. This is great sport and an enjoyable way to work a dog on a bird that generally sits very tight. Checking the DIF&W website will show you the locations of the release sites. These are on private land, for the most part, so hunters must be on their best behavior, respect signage and keep the areas clean of trash.

Happy Hour Hunts

Rejoice, you lovers of autumn! Crimson leaves, cool nights and sunny days beckon us toward hidden covers and secluded marshes. If you hunt birds, this is your month. Your dog may argue this statement, but that's between the two of you.

Many falls ago, I was assigned to attend training at the police academy in mid-October. I was somewhat upset, because the week-long class would cut into my precious upland hunting season, especially since this would be my dog's first year in the woods. As the days' classes dragged by, I caught myself glancing out the classroom window, staring at the falling leaves outside. I was in the heart of Maine's grouse woods without a chance to hunt! During a break, a fellow classmate and I were talking about bird hunting. He remarked that we were missing out on the best part of the season, a sentiment that I shared all too well. With a stroke of genius, he suggested we bring our shotguns along and spend our lunch break in the nearby coverts. It seemed that he had been driving past some "birdy" looking abandoned orchards all week and the temptation was too great. The simple suggestion that we make the most out of our available time started a fall ritual for both of us. Whenever the chance arose, during a noontime break or after getting out of work in the afternoon, we would grab our gear and head out for a happy hour hunt.

If you commute to work, chances are that you could almost drive blindfolded, knowing all the curves in the road as intimately as you know the layout to your own home. But how often do you notice the landscape around your paved route? You may be driving by some wonderful hunting cover, or perhaps such cover is just a few hundred yards off the path you travel, just out of sight, but nonetheless present every time you pass by. Robert Frost wrote "...two roads diverged in a wood, and I took the one less traveled by, and that has made all the difference." The familiar lines in this poem ring true for the hunter seeking to make the most of a happy hour hunt.

October

    If you took out a map and plotted your journey to work, and if you travel at all through a rural area where hunting is allowed, chances are that you will pass by huntable cover. Take a look at that map in detail and examine all of the side roads and trails that lie between your job and your home. These "roads less traveled" are oftentimes an oasis for birds that you would otherwise overlook.

    Once you've identified some potential hunting spots along your way to work, deciding when and how to hunt them is paramount. If your job allows it or if your supervisor is a hunter, you may be able to take off and hunt your new-found coverts whenever the urge arises. If you are like most of us, however, you probably don't have the luxury of that much freedom. Here's where the creative time manager shines. For some, an early morning grouse hunt when the sun is warming gravel paths and dew is still heavy on the leaves is the most favored time to hunt. If you prefer early morning grousing, arranging to arrive an hour or two late can provide you with beneficial exercise and put your mind in the proper frame for the rest of the day. Who wouldn't feel better starting each day with a bird hunt?

    Those who can't arrive late to work have two other options: leave early, or hunt at lunchtime. Many workplaces are forming wellness committees and workplace health programs. With a little explaining and a definite plan, you may be able to qualify for time allowances to hunt birds (and get exercise) during your noontime break. If your job is close to an undeveloped area where hunting is allowed, allowing for a few minutes travel time to and from your covert will give you a solid half- to three-quarters of an hour to hunt during a standard hour lunch period. You can even carry a snack to munch on the way to prevent a growling stomach from interrupting an important meeting. During midday, grouse are still busy feeding or sunning themselves, so a jaunt through the woods after the morning hunters have pushed a piece can oftentimes prove to be very productive.

    If you can't squeeze in your foray before or during the workday, leaving early can be a convincible option, even for the most stalwart boss. Many firms allow their employees to leave early by using partial vacation time or by converting overtime to compensatory time. If that is not available where you work, perhaps you can convince your boss to allow you to come in to work early and leave early. Not only will you avoid the rush hour traffic, you can hunt during the quiet of late afternoon and ambush birds on their way to their roosts or those getting their final feeding of the day. On frosty fall mornings when the temperature is below freezing, birds will often wait until the midday sun warms their trails before becoming active to any great extent. The afternoon hunter has the advantage on these chilly preludes to winter.

Whether you opt for a late start on the work day, a mid-day break to chase biddies or you head out after work for a few hours of solitude and splendor in the autumn woods, happy hour hunting is a concept whose time has come for the modern sportsman. Just be sure to take some time off and enjoy yourself!

A Cold Snap

Rene and I were bird hunting one chilly October morning. As per our usual routine, we fueled up on breakfast and drove north to our hunting grounds in the Rangeley region.

My lab, Luke, was in his prime and was a ball of fire. To say he was rambunctious was an understatement. But he had a good nose and could flush, find and retrieve anything.

We got to our first cover and I parked and let Luke out. He began racing back and forth like the wild thing he was. Rene got out to relieve himself and was standing in the overgrown twitch road where we would hunt, doing his business. The road had dozens of alder whips growing up in the middle of it, like most classic bird trails.

Luke ran past me and when he went by Rene, I heard Rene yell an expletive that one would not utter in a church. I turned to look and saw Luke coming back the other way. I saw exactly what the cause of Rene's consternation was, as the process repeated itself right before my very eyes.

As Luke rocketed past Rene, his chest bent an alder whip over and it ran underneath his belly. When he cleared it, it sprung upright, only to catch Rene on his exposed parts. The same curse came from Rene's mouth, but I'm certain it was both louder and higher pitched. I doubled over laughing, and Rene muttered something about how this injury had occurred twice, once in each direction. Rene has relayed this story a number of times, and it's funny every time I hear it. Apparently, the cold air served to magnify the pain as I'm certain happens to construction workers who bang their thumb with a hammer while working outdoors in the winter. Luke continued with the hunt as if nothing had happened. I can't recall how many birds we bagged or exactly where we were, but I'll never forget that visual!

A Dog's Taste

Another humorous tale involving Luke and Rene took place one October during moose season near Moosehead Lake. We were staying at George Belmont's place at Northeast Carry. Despite knowing that there would be moose hunters riding the roads, we decided to get in some bird hunting. The plan was to work the grown-up side roads off the main thoroughfares.

I pulled over and parked at the first likely spot we came to and let Luke out of the truck. He immediately went into the brush a few feet off the road. I hurriedly chambered two shells in my 20-gauge, knowing he was onto a bird. But nothing flushed. Luke was bent over in the brush, so I went in to inspect the situation. I yelled "leave it" but Luke wouldn't budge. Usually food or a bird is the only thing to anchor him that tight. I grabbed his collar and pulled him away as he was working to swallow something. I swept his mouth with my finger and at the same time I saw the white toilet paper on the ground. Wiping my hands on the grass, I scolded Luke and back in the truck we went. I'm sure Rene was chuckling a bit at my misfortune. He owed me, after all.

The next grown-up side road we came to looked promising, so we repeated the process. Luke repeated his performance, as well. Apparently, another hunter (I assume) did the same thing in this spot. What were the odds? This time Luke wanted to finish his "treat." I was seething when I finally got him and put his leash on him.

Now some dogs eat cat poop. Some dogs eat deer poop. Some even eat their own poop. I always bragged that Luke left those things alone. I guess he developed this taste later in life.

As we were riding back after a full day of hunting, Rene chuckled, shook his head and said, "That dog of yours is frigged up." Luke was curled up on the floor of my truck at Rene's feet, as he always did. He was sleeping with his muzzle on Rene's lap, a cute sight. Rene was asleep, as well, tired from the day's hunt. I saw Luke lift his head up and belch, expelling the contents of his stomach on Rene's lap. I know who had the last laugh that day.

Waterfowling, a Romance Sport

I would argue that there is, perhaps, no sport more romantic than waterfowling. Countless artists have captured that magical period just before sunrise, where hunter and dog wait pensively in a blind, fog settling just above the surface of the water. There is a chill in the air and the leaves have turned to crimson shades. Hunters set out decoys that have possibly been handed down through the generations and cradle guns that were once held by fathers or grandfathers.

Dogs, with their regrettably short lives come and go, each one holding a special spot in their owner's heart. I could go on, but it's time to set aside the sentimentality and get down to business—we have some duck hunting to do.

While bird hunters can place their bead on grouse, woodcock or perhaps pheasants, waterfowl hunters have a virtual cornucopia of targets to try for. We are all used to seeing the mallards—those are the ones that have green heads (the male of the species, anyway—or the black ducks, where both genders have a mottled brown appearance, but there are dozens of other waterfowl breeds and many make their way to Maine in the fall. Those of us who hunt ducks come to expect several of these varieties depending on time of month and hunting location.

The author after a successful waterfowl hunt with his old canoe and his old dog.

During the past several seasons that I can recall, the beautiful and diminutive green-winged teal has been a frequent visitor to my duck spots, especially in the early part of the month. Aside from its vibrant plumage, the green-winged teal is revered for its fast-flying antics and the difficulty it presents to the shooter. In years past when Maine had a special September teal season, hordes of these ducks passed through the state during their fall migration. Now, hunters rejoice when a brace of teal lands amongst their decoy spread. I have found most of my teal in small flowages and marshes that can provide plenty of cover for these shy ducks.

A few years ago, a group of my friends set up shop along the shoreline of The Basin in Auburn on opening day. They were intent on the abundant wood ducks and mallards that they had seen during frequent September scouting missions. Among the group were three recruits to the sport on their first duck hunt. After the hunters set up decoys for wood ducks and mallards, a pair of teal paid an early morning visit to their spread. Once the sun came up and the ducks saw where they were sitting, it was too late, as one of the neophyte hunters bagged his first trophy—a plump hen green-winged teal.

A young Adam Letourneau shows off his first duck taken while hunting with the author. Tom has introduced numerous youngsters, and some older sports, to the world of hunting and fishing in the great state of Maine.

Another equally pretty and even more abundant early season visitor to many marshes and ponds in the region is the wood duck. This small colorful duck inhabits bodies of water that are near its favorite food, acorns. In years when acorns are plentiful, the wood duck seems to fill the early October sky. My first duck was a drake (male) woodie taken while hunting along the Pushaw Stream in Old Town. I downed him with that old 16-gauge. I saved a black and white striped flank feather from that duck and still have it among my hunting and fishing treasures.

Several seasons ago, during a bountiful acorn crop, I took my daily limit of woodies on almost every outing. No matter where I hunted, I saw these gorgeous ducks. There were so many acorns that year that when they fell from the trees surrounding the water, it sounded like it was raining! The perfect wood duck spot is a marsh or pond ringed with oak trees. Early season scouting will provide the hunter with an idea of the best spot to ambush these fast-flying birds, but almost any spot along the shore will pay off.

Another top wood duck spot in my area, thanks to the efforts of those who install and maintain wood duck nesting boxes, is the Nezinscot River in Turner. The Nezinscot also sports the oak-lined shores that woodies adore. Several seasons past, Kevin Mulherin, now the Chief of Police in Monmouth, and I planned a mini float trip down the Nezinscot to hunt ducks. We put in near Buckfield and floated down into Turner. During the three-mile trip, we flushed dozens of wood ducks, as well as mallards, and enjoyed the beautiful scenery along the way. By paddling slowly and probing each cove, we were able to get in quite a bit of gunning during our four-hour journey. One word of caution, however, is that there are several camps alongside the river, and hunters should use care if they are not familiar with the area. If you have a wide, slow-flowing river in your neck of the woods, chances are you can enjoy a similar float hunt.

Rene mans the front of the canoe and scans for ducks as the author paddles him into one of their favorite hunting spots.

October

For hunters after the biggest thrill waterfowling holds, Canada goose hunting starts in September with an early season, running through December (depending on which zone you hunt). Geese spend time in corn fields and grassy spots to feed and then retreat to the water. Accordingly, hunters can set up in fields or on the water with decoys. Geese are extremely wary and thorough concealment is a must. The early season was established as a way to control nuisance geese that were turning up on lawns and golf courses, eating the grass and producing tons of waste. Geese in some states have caused public beach closures due to their waste products! Other hunters may journey north for grouse hunting or to the coastal rivers and marshes to do their waterfowling, but I prefer to stay close to home and enjoy the surprise of the variety of waterfowl available on local lakes, ponds and rivers.

A Blind Retrieve

Many hunters will brag that their duck dog will do blind retrieves. With the aid of the hunter's signals, the dog will go out and locate a bird that they did not see fall. Watching a dog trained for blind retrieves at a field trial or while hunting is impressive.

One crisp October morning, Rene and I were in our favorite spot and the ducks were flying. We were on the edge of a very productive marsh and I had strung a large piece of leaf-o-flage between two saplings. This served to hide us and the dog from the wary ducks.

I always kept Luke steadied by attaching his leash to the tree next to us, so he would not break when we started shooting. There was nothing he loved to do more than to swim after a downed duck, except for maybe chasing down a crippled bird.

We shot at three mallards, and dropped two. As was our practice, I unsnapped Luke from his leash and off he went. This time he decided that going *through* the blind was faster than going *around* it, so he charged headfirst into the perforated blind material. His head exploded through the canvas as the twine holding the blind to the tree stretched and finally broke away. Out he swam, wearing a camouflage shawl that was ten feet long. He resembled Superman in his cape—a little.

The author's Lab, Luke, sits patiently, this time, in the blind while awaiting ducks.

I was worried that the weight of the blind would drag him down and possibly drown him, so I immediately went toward my canoe, but upon watching him closely, I saw that it barely slowed him down. He got to the first duck and gently put his mouth around it, turned and swam back. I could see his strokes were a little labored, but soon he was on shore with the duck and my blind. I pulled the blind over his head and he charged out after the second duck as if nothing ever happened. Rene got quite a kick out of that show, as did I.

Moose Hunting

As we rounded a curve on a dirt road north of Oquossoc, I remarked to friend and hunting partner Bill Murphy that I would "love to see a shootable moose in the road." The words had no sooner escaped my lips when Murphy slowed the truck and exclaimed, "Shootable moose, shootable moose!" Because of the curve in the roadway, I couldn't see what he was looking at.

I stepped out of the truck, loaded my rifle and walked toward the middle of the roadway. Then I spotted a beautiful bull standing smack in the middle of the road. Seventy yards away, he was broadside, steam blowing out his nostrils. I stepped closer, took a kneeling stance and centered the crosshairs high on his shoulder. I took the shot, and the moose dropped out of sight, due to the slight hump in the road he was behind. I quickly walked up the roadway as sub-permittee Rene Lavoie loaded up to act as my backup, should we need a follow-up shot.

When we reached the moose, a beautiful bull with a 49-inch spread and wide palms, there was no need for backup. The moose was down, right in the middle of the dirt road. Two hours later he was hanging at River's Edge Sports in Oquossoc, weighing in at 725 pounds. The cleaning, loading and chilling of the moose could not have gone smoother, thanks in part to the location where he dropped and our preparation and gear selection.

Tom and Rene teamed up in 2012 to bag this beautiful bull moose above Oquossoc.

October

This same trio of hunters tagged a cow moose in 2000, so we knew what we needed to take and had more gear than necessary, just in case. When it comes to handling one of North America's largest game animals, preparation and the right equipment are crucial to ending a successful hunt on a positive note.

Let's face it; most of us head out into the deer woods with little more equipment than a knife to gut our prize and a string to tie on the transport tag. Moose, because of their sheer size, require far more equipment than is necessary for deer. Each season, ill-prepared moose hunters waste meat and trophies because they aren't geared up for the challenge. Planning your hunt to address field dressing, loading and transporting your moose not only saves you time and effort, it ensures the game meat is table-ready—an honor due the majestic moose.

With the moose down, Rene and I went to work while Bill videotaped our progress and provided some humorous commentary (see "Tom's Maine Moose Hunt 2012" on YouTube). Our first order of business was getting dressed for the task at hand. We each donned a set of rain bib overalls to protect our pants from the inevitable blood and entrails. The paunch of a moose is the size of a small cow, so moving it around is no small task. Shoulder-length plastic gloves, with several pairs at the ready in case of a tear, protected our arms and sleeves. Next, we readied several knives, as the hair and hide on a moose quickly dull a blade. Any of the field dressing knives with replaceable razor-type blades would be a perfect choice for this task, as you can discard the blade as it dulls. Then, we used the surveyor's twine I carried along to tie off the bladder and intestines to prevent their contents from spoiling any meat. Finally, a Wyoming saw was used to split the brisket all the way up to the neck to remove the entire windpipe and cool the carcass as much as possible.

I wasn't planning a neck mount, so sawing the cape up to the throat was not an issue. If you are contemplating a shoulder mount, consult your taxidermist and do not cut the cape all the way up. A Wyoming saw has a bone and wood blade, folds compactly and stores in a nice leather sheath. It's a handy tool to have

October

with you on any trip into the woods. Once the carcass was drained, we packed it with frozen milk bottles, making certain to fill the entire cavity. We used both gallon and half gallon sizes, enabling us to quickly chill the meat.

Getting a moose into the back of a pick-up truck or onto a trailer is no small feat. If you are lucky enough to drop a moose on a dirt road near a logging operation, many times a wood cutter will use a skidder or log loader to haul out and load your quarry for you. A generous cash tip for diesel or gasoline would always be appreciated and is a nice gesture. Without such equipment at your disposal, you should be ready to move an object weighing up to half a ton.

Having two moose under my belt, I was lucky and smart enough to drop each one on a dirt road. I passed up shots on moose standing 100 yards in a clear cut, knowing that pulling moose out of a stump and slash-infested cutting would be next to impossible. However, if you find your moose in a more remote location, one technique works very well for dragging your trophy out of the woods.

I was watching a video of a Maine moose hunter twitching his kill out of the woods using a capstan winch. The capstan winch is a gas-powered device the size of a chainsaw power head that uses a rope and friction to pull a heavy load. You may have seen one on a lobster boat, as they are commonly used to bring in lobster traps. This version is gas-powered and portable. Just anchor it to a tree or stump, and pull away.

Even more interesting than watching the winch work was how the moose was prepared. The hunter had an old truck bed liner that he rolled the moose into, and the slipperiness of the bed liner allowed the moose to slide easily over brush, slash and uneven terrain. I went to a local salvage yard and bought a liner from an 8-foot truck for fifty dollars. Even though my moose needed little hauling, the bed liner made the moose slide effortlessly onto my trailer. Just roll the moose into the liner and tie the sides together, enveloping the moose, similar to how Native Americans wrapped buckskin around their travois when hauling things by hand or by horse.

We used a four-wheeler to pull the moose onto my trailer. These devices are indispensable when hunting moose. They can be used to quietly scout for your quarry, drag it out of the woods and then finally winch it onto a trailer. We even used the weight of the machine to hold one of the hind legs apart during the field dressing operation.

On our first hunt, we managed to get the 600-pound cow I harvested into the back of my full-sized pick-up truck. Using another truck to pull a rope draped over the bedrail (protected by a boat cushion), we pulled the cow up a pair of wooden ramps. This was a difficult task, as a moose doesn't follow a set of narrow ramps easily. I remarked to my hunting partners that I would bring a utility trailer if we ever drew a moose permit again. This time, I brought along my trailer, a 7-foot by 12-foot model. This easily fit my moose and four-wheeler, leaving the bed of the truck free for myriad other gear. The beauty about having a trailer along for the hunt is that you can do as we did and park it with the four-wheeler on it and drive around until both are needed. As soon as my bull was on the ground, Rene and I went to work field dressing it while Bill went back for the trailer and four-wheeler. My utility trailer proved ideal, but even an open snowmobile trailer or a smaller utility trailer will hold a moose.

Other critical items to have on a moose hunt, and items that I lugged along were: a chainsaw to assist with clearing a path to your moose; spare tires (at least two if riding on shale or dirt roads); a good jack (if you need to use one of those spares); plenty of rope; and a clean tarp. Fortunately, we didn't need any of these items, but if we had, they were better to have along than if they were still in my garage back home. Despite the high success rate for the Maine moose hunt and the large number of moose taken alongside a dirt road, moose hunters should be prepared for a difficult extraction. Having the proper gear not only makes the hunt more enjoyable, it ensures a quality product on the table, honoring the animal and the hunt for years to come. Of course, having a

October

good friend like Bill Murphy with a camp and access to a large wilderness area was paramount to both our success and the enjoyment of those hunts.

October comes to a close too soon. Most hunters won't run their bird dogs during deer season, so for them, 31 days is brutally short. But cheer up! Hunters' breakfasts are being advertised, "Game Tagging Station" signs are being affixed to the mom and pop stores, and everyone is getting antsy. It's November, and that means deer season!

November

Deer Season Dominates November

As a youngster growing into hunting age, all I had on my mind were visions of pheasants exploding from a cornfield or a grouse rocketing through a hardwood stand. Oh, and of course, a morning spent on the marsh hunting ducks. My dad was a bird hunter, so those are the stories I was told. As I got older and went away to college, I decided it was time I started deer hunting, so I bought a used Marlin 336C chambered in .30-30 Winchester. I was now a deer hunter, or so I thought.

I headed off to college with my entire arsenal: that .30-30, my 16-gauge pump and a single-shot .410. The campus police at the University of Maine had a great program for hunters. You could store your firearms at the police department and sign them out to hunt. I am told the same system still exists. This novel approach keeps the firearms safe but accessible.

I would check out my rifle when I had a morning or afternoon off and roam the woods of Hudson or Alton or another nearby wooded spot. I had a few buddies who hunted deer, so we would often head out and meet up later for lunch or to report back any sightings. I shot at one massive buck, my first ever, but buck fever had me shaking and I missed an easy shot. He was trailing a doe with his nose to the ground and never saw me until I fired from a mere 30 feet away. That same morning, my classmate, Jeff Davis, took a shot at a spike-horn buck and was convinced he had missed. After we determined I missed my deer, we went to double-check for his. Sure enough, it had dropped in the gully by an old culvert on a logging trail and he found him! We both agreed it would have been an even better morning had I got my deer, as well. To this day I replay that muffed shot in my head.

The biggest deer I have ever seen in person fell to my roommate, Scott Wentzel, of Pennsylvania. Scott, Jeff Davis and I were hunting our favorite spot one year and had split up. Late in the afternoon I heard a shot, followed by a few more. There were other hunters in the area so I didn't think it was either of my two buddies. After about an hour, as it got close to the end of legal hunting, I heard more shots and then Jeff shouting. I walked toward the noise and soon came upon Jeff walking out. He was disheveled and exclaimed that Scott had shot a monster buck. We met up with Scott and he relayed his tale.

He saw the huge buck and fired at it quickly. If memory serves me, he had an old British .303 bolt action rifle. His first shot broke the deer's front leg and when it turned he fired again, this time paunching the deer. As he hurried toward the deer, he lost the spare shells that he had jammed into the shotgun shell loops of his vest. He tracked the deer toward a swamp and got another shot off, only to realize he had now run out of ammo. Jeff heard the commotion and went his way. Jeff caught up to Scott and assisted in tracking the deer. I don't recall if Scott took Jeff's gun or Jeff fired, but more rounds of buckshot from Jeff's single-shot 12-gauge were sent into the deer, finally killing it. There was an old farmhouse down across from the access road we were on, so we walked out to see if they had a three-wheeler (four-wheelers weren't very common back then). The old grizzled resident of the farmhouse said he would assist and fired up a decrepit snowmobile. Despite the fact that there was no snow on the ground, he drove it in the woods to help us drag out Scott's prize. When we got to the deer, I could not believe the rack and the size of the deer. It was a beautiful 12-pointer that would weigh in at 227 pounds. Quite a trophy for a college student, or any hunter, for that matter.

When Scott plunged his knife into the abdomen to start the field dressing process, the stench of stomach contents wafted up to all our noses. The old-timer exclaimed, "Smells like an old, dead twat!" We got quite a chuckle out of that statement and repeated it often through our college years.

Tom's First Deer

During my senior year, one of my roommates, Mike Brown from Bath, suggested we leave school early on a Friday and hunt out of his family camp in Corinna. Mike described the camp as rustic and said it was in the heart of farm country with lots of deer. He didn't have to twist my arm.

We stopped for provisions on the way and rolled into camp as it was getting dark. The camp was rustic but well-suited to the task at hand. I remember the icebox as nothing more than a hole cut in the camp wall with a wooden box attached to the outside with holes for ventilation—a novel idea. Mike made a great meal with baked chicken and green beans, and we were off to bed early to get up before light.

Most camps have some mice, and this one was no different. But these mice liked to mess with us. As I lay in my sleeping bed, the mice raced across me at breakneck speeds. I'm not afraid of mice, so I chalked it up to deer camp life and finally got to sleep. When we awoke, Mike made a hearty breakfast and gave me my instructions.

Since I didn't know the woods, I was to walk down a woods road and find a spot to sit, watching the woods to the north. I crept down the road in the dark and when I gauged I was in a good spot, I found a hemlock to sit against and waited for the sun to rise.

It was cold in mid-November, so the sun felt good. I sat and scanned the woods around me for any sign of deer, but none appeared. The cold settled in and around 9:00 a.m. I had to get up and walk to get my blood pumping. Mike told me the road ended in a field, so I decided I'd walk there. After a few minutes walking and scanning the woods, I saw the opening to the field ahead of me. It had recently been tilled and I saw a large pile of potatoes at the edge of it, probably damaged from the harvester. I saw a wide trail coming from the woods into the field and surmised it must be a game trail.

I looked in all directions and didn't see a farm or house and turned to look back toward the woods. The deer caught me by surprise. It wasn't there a moment ago, and then there it stood. I lay down on a dirt mound and the deer, standing out about 80 yards from me, looked at me, but went back to eating something from the field. It was a doe, so I used my rifle scope to scan the wood line for a buck. Nothing. I looked at the deer as it munched on a potato and saw it was actually a buck, with one antler busted off and a small crotch horn on the other side.

Elated it was a buck, legal quarry for me, I cocked the hammer back and aimed. I felt that buck fever creep in again, but I steadied myself and regained my composure. I put the crosshairs just behind the front shoulder and squeezed the trigger. The buck dropped where it once stood. I was a deer hunter!

I rushed up to my prize and tied my tag around the remaining antler and began field dressing it. I had helped Jeff with his deer, so I knew the process. As I was getting ready to make the long drag home, a man pulled up in the adjacent field and yelled, "Is that what's been eating your carrots?" I walked over to him and he was surprised to see I was not his farmer neighbor. I introduced myself and told him where I was staying and he kindly offered to drive me to tag my deer and drop me off at camp. Talk about the kindness of strangers. I bought the guy his pack of smokes while the clerk filled out my tag at the little country store. On the ride back to camp we came upon my buddy Mike walking toward the cabin and he was surprised to see me in a truck, with a deer no less. He remarked that he thought I must have gotten lost, but nothing was further from the truth. That hunt sticks in my memory, and I can't help but go back to it every year before opening day. I learned the value of watching the edge where field meets forest that November morning.

The author and his first deer taken during his college years.

Hunt the Edges for Deer

As the sun slowly disappeared below the tree line in front of me, that eerie period before dark, where all is still, gradually moved in. Only five minutes remained until legal shooting time was up, and the plan was to stay at my stand until the end. No sooner had I looked up from my watch, when the deer appeared. Two does jumped from the wooded edge through the narrow band of marsh grass. They casually fed on the lush field grass, just

November

80 yards in front of me. A well-aimed shot took the lead doe as she turned broadside. Deer season was over for another year, and I had tender venison for the freezer.

The practice of stand hunting the edge between habitat types is as old as the sport itself, but many sportsmen don't realize the theory behind this practice, and why it attracts deer. Biologists and naturalists have studied these "ecotones" or "edges" in detail and have concluded that richness in species diversity and species numbers is often greatest where the food and cover requirements of a species come together.

All states have several types of edge habitat, consisting of both man-made and natural edges. Man-made edge habitats include farm fields meeting a wood line, strip cuts, clear cuts and zones where prescribed burns meet existing vegetation. Natural edge habitat occurs where different ecosystems meet such as a hardwood ridge meeting a softwood stand, or more commonly, as a result of a short-term environmental disturbance such as a wildfire, flood or erosion. With these descriptions in mind, it's not very difficult to reflect on your favorite hunting area and place the topography into one category or another.

During my college years, we hunted a piece of land in Hudson, Maine, that was a textbook example of the variety of edge types. As you entered the woods from the road, you walked uphill through a dense plot of eastern white pine. At the top of the hill, the appearance of the forest changed drastically as the pine stand was halted abruptly by a hardwood ridge of beech and oak. Next, after passing easterly through the hardwoods, you came to a field. Rows of apple trees, long neglected and sparse on fruit, lined the rock wall that bordered the southern edge of the field. The grass had grown up into tall weeds, and occasionally a lone maple or alder sapling would stand out in the field of grass. As you walked downhill toward a lake, you entered a series of three alder fields, each in a different stage of succession.

My college roommates and I took a bounty of grouse, woodcock and rabbits from this land of many edges, and saw countless deer and deer sign. As a wildlife student, I recalled thinking about the different types of edges that were present there, and at the other places that we hunted, as well. When scouting out a new area to hunt deer, the importance of hunting these edges is always on my mind.

Deer flock to this edge habitat for a variety of reasons. A field meeting a forest provides ruminants, like deer, with essential grasses to feed on. Deer love clover and rye, and will oftentimes come out in the daytime to feed on these delicious treats. You will usually see a doe and her fawns enter the field first. The buck waits in the security of the thick trees that line the field to wait and see if it's safe to come out in the open. So, in this sense, the edge habitat also provides essential cover for the white-tailed deer. Hunters in farm country know this rule, and often wait all afternoon from a comfortable vantage point to take a shot at a deer with a scoped rifle. I've used this technique when hunting a field that is out of sight from the road.

Most rural areas have farms that have "back fields." Get to know the farmer and ask permission to set up a stand or blind and stay until the end of legal shooting time. Deer are oftentimes lulled into the false sense of security that a remote field provides. Another popular technique for hunting field edges involves doing a bit of detective work and finding the trail that the deer are using to get to the field. By backtracking it and ambushing the deer before they reach the field, you can often take the wise old buck that won't step out in the open until sundown.

Hunters in areas of the country where forest harvesting is abundant know the value of hunting the edges, as well. Take a walk out into a strip-cut or clear-cut area a few months after the wood has been harvested. Deer literally come out of the woodwork to feed on the tender shoots that blossom from the stumps of cut trees. By scanning the edges where the cutting stopped, you can often get a glimpse of a big buck as he peers across the harvested area for danger before making a suppertime appearance. If you've done your homework and located the trails where the deer enter and leave the cutting, you should be able to set your stand up at a spot to cover the deer's approach route and intercept one on their way to feed. While some may argue against clear-cutting practices, strip cutting is perhaps one of the best ways to create edge habitat for deer and other game and non-game species.

Rene shows off his 2019 8-pointer.

If you've ever been into the woods after a forest fire or a prescribed burn, you know how desolate the forest can look. Charred logs, layers of soot and blackened trees create an eerie picture that is most depressing to a hunter or wildlife lover. Return to that same plot over the next few years, however, and you will be pleasantly surprised. While there will still be evidence of the fire all around, you'll probably see an abundance of new vegetation and growth, along with an abundance of deer sign. By locating a recently burned area and scouting the fringe areas of the fire, you should find deer trails into the smorgasbord of greens and shoots. Again, set up your stand so that you can cover as much of the area as possible, concentrating on the entrance trails near the edge of the burn.

Aldo Leopold, the founder of our country's game management profession, wrote that "Game is a phenomenon of the edges, wildlife occurs where the types of food and cover which it needs come close together." By recognizing the many places in your state where edge habitat occurs, and taking a stand on these edges, you should have no trouble seeing or taking deer as they make their way to these food and cover bonanzas.

Dress to Impress

I always laugh when I see photos of hunters in Maine from the 1800s. They are often dressed in three-piece wool suits or other fancy regalia. How impractical that type of clothing must have been. Well, that's what I thought until I found myself in a similar situation.

It was mid-November 1990 and I was working night shift. I had court on Tuesday morning at 8:30 a.m. so I stayed up after work and threw my suit on and headed into court. I had hunted the day before, so my gun and orange vest were still in my truck. I recall the suit, a gray flannel model with a vest. I was probably the best-dressed cop in court, but my defendant didn't show up, so I was released by 9:00 a.m. I drove out Summer Street headed to my North Auburn house. The firearms discharge rules that they have in Auburn now weren't in effect then, so outer Summer Street was open to hunting. As I made my way past a field, I saw a deer standing there about 30 yards off the road! It all happened so quickly. I knew I had my gun and orange vest and hat, I had

November

my rifle and shells and I was in an open area. I slowed my truck down and planned on how I would get all these items together to be legal and get a shot at this deer, a large doe. I couldn't believe she was still standing there.

I pulled to a stop and she trotted into the woods about 100 yards ahead of me, still close to the road. I knew there was a woods road just down from where she went into the tree line, so I headed there. I parked, got out, threw on my orange and loaded my rifle. I still remember looking down at my cordovan-colored wing-tip shoes and thinking I was crazy. I quietly closed my truck door and walked down the grown-up road. I was no more than 50 yards into the woods when I saw her. She was standing behind a tree, but with enough of her shoulder exposed to aim at. Knowing I had precious little time before she bolted, I cocked my .30-30, aimed and fired. She dropped right there.

I was quite happy, as she was only my second deer. I walked over to my prize and saw her left front leg was broken and twisted with shards of bone sticking out. Now I knew why she wasn't running off at high speed. It was evident that she had been hit by a car and it was a blessing that I was able to end any suffering. I reached into my hunting vest and pulled out the adhesive doe tag they used to issue and tagged her. That's when I realized there was one thing missing—my hunting knife. My house was just up the road and the tagging station, Sheldon Savage's old North Auburn Cash Market, was just past that. I dragged the plump doe to my truck and dropped the tailgate. I was in my prime, so I was strong enough to swing the doe into the bed, but I was worried about getting blood on my suit. Instead, I stood in the bed holding her good front leg and pulled her up into the truck. Not a drop of blood got on me, and I was off.

Not wanting to dress the deer in my suit or show up dressed like that at the tagging station, I quickly changed into jeans and an old shirt. I dressed the doe and tagged her and then I was off to the butcher. All of this before noon. I was able to catch a good nap and had quite the story to tell that night at work. I also learned that a motorist called in a late report, saying they had hit a deer in the wee hours of the morning, but it had run off. The deer was in perfect shape, except for the busted leg and was good eating. I can safely say I have never looked so sharp in the woods!

Deer Butchers

Practitioners of a nice cottage industry, local deer butchers put up signs on telephone poles and in front of their homes each fall, advertising their craft for lucky hunters. I have cut up several of my deer, but find it easier to let a professional handle the task. Years ago, a local fur buyer would set up shop each fall and trade hunters for their deer hides. One deer hide fetched a brand new pair of insulated deerskin gloves. I sported a new pair every season I got a deer!

For quite some time now, I have been going to the same butcher, Dave Finocchietti Sr. of Gray. I worked with his son, Dave Jr., who introduced me to his dad. We took an immediate liking to each other. My grandfather was a butcher, so I always have had a soft spot for that profession. Dave Sr. loved police patches, so I gave him many of those I had picked up over the years. Over time, Dave would allow me to work alongside him and butcher my own deer, something I truly enjoy. Nothing beats having a professional give you tips. I look forward to seeing Dave each November, if I'm lucky.

The coming colder months are perfect for cooking venison chili before the big football game or putting a deer shoulder roast in the crockpot before work, only to return home to the smell of pot roast and fall vegetables simmering in gravy. That is, if you filled your tag!

December

Another Year Winds Down

December is a busy month because of family gatherings and holiday celebrations. Deer hunters in southern Maine get two more weeks for muzzleloader season, and that seems to be becoming more popular among my hunting friends. If I haven't tagged out after four weeks in November, I am not excited about hunting in December with a gun that shoots only once, but that's me. Plenty of smokepole hunters would gladly hunt an extra two weeks.

Hunters can still chase grouse and small game this month, too. I went on a winter grouse hunt in the snow a few seasons back, and we did see some birds. "See" was the operative word, because these birds were skittish! Buddies Greg Hamilton and John Desjardins and I went up around Eustis to chase some late season biddies. We drove the roads since there was little snow that year, and managed to see a few birds roosting in the sun, but they flushed as soon as we stopped the truck. I guess after a few months of being gunned at, they get shy. But if you haven't got your fill of hunting yet, a December sea duck hunt is great sport.

Cold Duck

Sitting low in the boat as it bobbed off the coast, I could see a flock of scoters just off the water headed toward our decoys. Rene saw them too, so when I hollered, "Take 'em," he started shooting. I fired twice and dropped one, and Rene had two down in the water. This was sea duck hunting, a hardy and exciting sport that every hunter needs to experience.

Shells fly as sea duck hunters get some fast and furious shooting in.

With deer season over and ice fishing season dependent on cold temperatures for making ice, the anxious outdoors person can still get in on an exciting cold weather sport: sea duck hunting. Once a sport enjoyed by a few stalwart souls such as lobstermen who made their living on the water and had a sturdy boat, the popularity of sea duck hunting has risen steadily, with Maine being one of the top sea duck hunting destinations in the world.

Open until mid-January, the sea duck season provides hunters with ample opportunity to take advantage of mild winter days and

December

abundant bag limits. Sea duck hunters are allowed to bag a daily limit of five birds. Of the five birds, no more than four can be scoters, nor can hunters bag more than four eiders or long-tailed ducks.

Maine is often touted as the sea duck capital of the northeast. Although the title is well deserved, Maine is tailor made for sea duck hunting. Including all of the state's bays, inlets and coastal islands, Maine has more than 3,500 miles of coastline that serve as shelter for ducks and hunters alike.

According to Maine Department of Inland Fisheries and Wildlife Biologist Brad Allen, there are so many potential hot spots for sea duck action that if you picked almost any spot on the map from Castine down to Casco Bay, you would be in prime sea duck habitat for a variety of species. With Maine taking more than half the national harvest of sea ducks, it's no wonder that hunters are flocking to the Pine Tree state to get in on this action.

Allen was quick to point out that for sea duck hunters, the southern portion of the state is the best place to go, particularly the Casco Bay region. "Casco Bay is very popular among waterfowlers for three reasons: you have great access to the water, there are plenty of local accommodations, and the resource in that part of the state is doing quite well."

Novices to the sport are best advised to seek the services of a guide or go with an experienced sea duck hunter before venturing out alone. Although the waters around the Maine coastline are typically calmer than the open ocean, tides, swells, ledge and other hazards do exist to make this sport more demanding than inland duck hunting.

Hunters should be in a stable craft, preferably 16 feet or greater. A deep vee boat is preferred for its ability to cut through waves and handle rough water. My hunting partner, Rene, uses a 16-foot deep vee boat with a 40-horsepower outboard. He also carries along a small outboard, just in case the big one quits. Hunting equipment can be as simple as a string of bleach bottles for decoys or as sophisticated as several strings of cork decoys representing eiders or scoters.

Rene guns at an incoming flock of sea ducks off the coast of Maine.

A 10- or 12-gauge shotgun with plenty of non-toxic shot (I take four boxes on each hunt) is necessary, as the heavy down of these hardy birds can absorb a lot of shot. My hunting partner and I anchor on the lee side of a small island and set out two strings of six decoys each and wait for the action. Sea ducks decoy well and ducks will often circle back after you have shot at the flock. Two anchors are necessary to keep the boat in position when the swells are heavy, and a camouflage net to cover the boat helps to conceal your location.

Waiting for a flock of eiders or scoters to come in is as much fun as waiting out a circling mallard when hunting inland with one difference. Instead of dropping in from a high flight pattern, sea ducks come in hard, fast and just off the surface of the water. Keeping your head down and peering over the rail of the boat helps locate incoming ducks, but these kamikazes of the ocean buzz in fast, requiring a healthy lead and follow-through.

December

A brace of eiders.

If you have the desire to get in some late season shooting in one of the most picturesque settings the state has to offer, a Maine coast sea duck hunt should satisfy your desire. Exercise caution, because the winter sea is as dangerous as it is beautiful, and no bird is worth one's life. Watch the weather forecast and choose a day with calm winds and light seas. If you play it safe and plan your trip accordingly, you can usher in the New Year by enjoying some of the best hunting that Maine has to offer.

Each End a Beginning

I never resent the ending of the year. Perhaps it is the sportsman in me that knows there is always another season ahead. I do wish we could stretch ice-out fishing and make it last longer on each lake. I'd also like October to be 62 days instead of 31. While I'm on this topic, I'd gladly give up daylight saving time, too, to get more daylight at the end of a winter day. It would be nice to come home from work and have some daylight left for chores or repairs. But, alas, we are all constrained by the vagaries of Congress.

Over the years I have learned to savor each month, each week, each day; and along with these, the year. I have found that preparing my tackle bag for ice-out trolling on a cold March day when the ice isn't safe enough to fish allows me to look forward to the coming season and reflect on seasons past. A missed shot at a grouse this fall will surely bring new chances next October. Cleaning a shotgun before bird season brings me back to the first time my grandfather showed me the process. That specific memory is triggered each and every time I catch a whiff of Hoppe's No. 9.

So, here we are at the end of another year. Or is it the start of a new one? To me, it's both. We can reflect on past sporting adventures and look forward to upcoming ones. Thank goodness Maine has so much to offer us in each month. I think that's the reason I keep my anchor here and only drift a bit.

A Traveling Sportsman

I've had the pleasure and fortune to hunt and fish in several states, Canada and the Caribbean. I'm no safari hunter, nor have I obtained any type of "slam" (unless you count the year I tagged a bear, a deer, and a moose). I think that's what makes me appreciate my adventures away from my home state that much more. Sit back with me while I reminisce on a few jaunts that continue to bring fond memories.

Caribou Adventure

As the Cessna banked and prepared to land on the unnamed lake, I could see three boats each with two hunters and a guide, starting out for their day afield. The flaps were set and we powered down until water grabbed the floats. The camp was directly in front of us and in minutes, Camp Manager Roland St. Pierre and his wife, Pauline, the cook, were on the dock greeting me. After my gear was unloaded and stored, I changed into my hunting clothes and met with Roland over a late breakfast. Roland thought it would be best if he showed me the blinds near camp first and then later we could hunt one of the blinds that were across the lake. I agreed, and we took a leisurely tour of the land around the camp.

All the blinds have a nickname, usually the name of a repeat customer who has spent time there or had unusual success from that particular spot. "Doc's blind" is the favorite spot of long-time client, the late Dr. Paul Beegle of Auburn. Doc Beegle was an accomplished outdoorsman and a frequent guest at Roland's camp. "The Sheraton" is reminiscent of the hotel of the same name, offering a large room with a great view.

Situated well into the tundra of Quebec, Luco Caribou Adventure managed a series of camps in the Caniapiscau region of northern Quebec. Luco is now out of business, as the caribou herd in that region declined so rapidly that the hunting season has been closed for the past few years. A sad commentary on the frailty of nature.

I was staying at Camp 6, which Roland himself built—quite an undertaking when you think that the only way to get materials into this vast land is by float plane. Inuits drag boats in on snowmobiles in the winter, but the float plane is the fastest way to get something to camp. The camp itself has great amenities, including a hot shower, a well-stocked kitchen with a great cook and a satellite phone available, but caribou were my biggest concern. I quickly realized that despite these extras, the camp's location made it a top destination for caribou hunters looking to score on one of North America's largest hoofed animals. This land is rugged with no trees taller than a man. The ground is lichen-covered granite.

Once our tour of the nearby blinds was over, Roland suggested we head across the lake and climb a steep ridge to the "Hilton blind." Roland's then 12-year-old grandson, Michael Lucas, came up with me for the adventure. I brought Michael on his first bird hunt, first duck hunt and even took him when he bagged his first deer, a nice eight-pointer. He was a good kid then and has grown into a solid, respectable young man. We loaded our gear into the camp boat and headed across the lake. After a short trip, we climbed up the steep hill to the blind. The Hilton blind is located on the top of a ridge that overlooks the lake, the camps and a huge meadow where the caribou migrate through. You can see for several hundred yards and judging from the droppings and tracks, the animals migrate right next to the blind, a perfect spot for bowhunters.

We determined that Michael would get the first shot, so we began the waiting process. The caribou follow repetitive migration patterns and move from 20 to 40 miles each day, eating along the way, in groups as small as one or two up to the thousands. Roland told me that when they arrived in camp to open it, several thousand caribou charged right through the camp, alongside the tents where the clients would soon be sleeping.

After about an hour, Roland whispered that there was a bunch of caribou grazing in the meadow below. Using binoculars, I was quickly able to spot them. Even at a distance of several hundred yards, these animals seemed huge! As Roland explained, the caribou would disappear briefly as they entered a stand of gnarled spruce and then suddenly reappear as they crested the ridge we were on. After a ten-minute wait, I saw a set of antlers with velvet hanging off one of the tips. Soon the rest of the animals came into view as he crested the hill. Several cows followed close behind and they moved our way. Michael steadied his gun and took aim at the lead bull that was still on the move. When the firing began, the herd became alarmed and began looking about, but this was not the same type of reaction you would get with a group of deer. These animals seemed more curious than frightened. Michael had exhausted his magazine, so, Roland gave me the nod. The bull I wanted had started to trot off, but at a leisurely pace. I judged his pace and led him slightly, dropping him with a neck shot. I had just shot my first caribou! The rest of the herd disappeared over the next hill and we began the process of dressing this magnificent animal.

As I approached him, I noted the bull seemed huge by Maine deer standards, both in body size and antler mass. It was those antlers that first caught my eye. I had just collected a beautiful example of a double-shovel rack that was well out of velvet.

"What a mount these antlers would make," I mused to myself as I helped Roland with the task at hand. Because of the size of these animals, weighing between 250 and 700 pounds on the hoof, they must be quartered. My experience with field dressing big game was limited to bear, deer and moose, so I was anxious to learn the tricks of the trade.

Michael Lucas with a caribou he took in northern Quebec.

The four quarters were quickly cut from the caribou. Roland handed me a saw and asked that I trim off the forelegs and hoofs. When I questioned him about this, he responded by saying, "You don't want to carry the extra weight, do you?" That made sense to me, so off they came.

The loins were still in the animal, so Roland showed me just how they remove these delicacies. To get the backstraps, Roland trimmed the hide off the animal's back and filleted the loins out in strips away from the ribs and backbone. To get to the inner tenderloins, Roland used his saw and cut through the backbone and ribcage, creating a flap. When he peeled the flap away from the body, the loins were attached to the bottom of the ribs alongside the backbone and were easily removed. Pretty slick.

Finally, the antlers were cut off by sawing through the skull plate. This gave us a set of hindquarters, a set of front quarters, two sets of loins and a rack to haul out. We each loaded a packframe with a front and hindquarter and packed the meat out, carrying the loins in a cheesecloth bag. I opted to carry the rack, so I could admire it on the hike down to the boat. Once back at camp, my meat was placed in the screened-in meat tent where the cool temperatures would keep it fresh until my departure.

That night, the whole camp celebrated as eight of us had taken our first caribou on the first day of the hunt. Roland awarded handsome pewter pins of a caribou bust to each of the lucky hunters. The following day I spent the morning in the same blind, but never saw an animal to fill my second tag.

The next day, I took Michael back to the Hilton blind and we hatched a plan. He would shoot his two caribou first, and then I would shoot my second. As the poet says, the best laid plans of mice and men do go astray, and this situation was no different. After spending an hour in the blind, I caught a glimpse of movement in the meadow below. Through my binoculars I could see a group of cows moving toward us. After waiting almost twenty minutes, I gave up hope, thinking they may have moved in a different direction. Caribou are the only members of the deer family where both sexes may have antlers, but not all cows sport antlers.

Almost instantly, a group of bulls crested the ridge and were headed in our direction. There were three bulls, one with a much larger rack than the others. I told Michael to take the big bull, and then shoot a second animal. I planned to wait until Michael was tagged out to take my second caribou. These caribou were walking directly toward our blind, getting closer with each step. When they were within 30 yards, I told Michael to shoot when he was ready. His first shot was at the big bull, but instead of dropping, he turned to trot away. Two more shots dropped the bull before he could make his retreat. His attention was now on another of the remaining two bulls, but that bull had run alongside the blind without offering a shot. While Michael watched it, I took the final bull that was looking directly at me. He dropped instantly and we began to celebrate. I took Roland's video camera and began to record Michael as we left the blind to claim our trophies, but to my dismay, my caribou was up and running away from us. I shouldered my rifle and sent three shots in his direction, dropping him on the last shot. Apparently my first shot had only stunned him.

The author with his handsome double-shovel caribou.

Roland could hear the shooting from camp and called us by radio to see how we had done. He was soon on his way to assist with the packing out of the meat. By the end of the week, the whole camp had tagged out on bulls and Luco Caribou Adventure ended their 2004 season a week later in October with a 100% success rate, a testimony to their location and the determination of the guides.

The guides were truly indispensable, providing the knowledge to get the clients to the game, pack the heavy meat out and ensure client safety while afield. As for the food, I was exhausted when I returned to camp after a full day of hunting on the tundra. What a welcome sight it was to see Pauline in the kitchen, laying out a meal fit for kings, knowing that I didn't have to start a fire and cook my own meal.

My caribou hunt was incredibly enjoyable and I relived those memorable events with each caribou steak that I grilled. Let's move over to another nearby Canadian province.

PEI Goose Hunt

As the west wind roared across the barley field, I pulled my collar up higher in a vain attempt to stop the chill. The rain that pelted my ears and neck seemed to be coming in sideways. I huddled down lower in hopes that the spruce boughs of the blind would cut the wind, but they did not.

Slowly, I began to hear a faint cry in the distance. The cry became louder until it sounded like a chorus of trumpeters. Our guide answered back with his song. I crouched down lower to avoid detection. All at once, the guide cried out, "Take 'em boys," and I sprang up. In front of me were five Canada geese, wings cupped above the decoys. They appeared to be suspended from the sky as they fought the wind to land. Upon seeing the commotion in the hedgerow, they reeled back in an attempt to gain altitude. Their attempts were too late and each hunter brought down one of these magnificent birds, considered to be the big game of waterfowl. While the weather would vary, the abundant geese were an almost constant and this scenario repeated itself numerous times over the years as I made a sojourn to visit what is arguably goose hunting Mecca, Prince Edward Island (PEI), Canada.

Located off the coast of New Brunswick, Canada, PEI is within a day's drive from New England. More importantly, PEI is one of the first stopover destinations for hundreds of thousands of geese as they migrate south for the winter. With near 100% success rates, reasonable hunting packages and a variety of other winged game, PEI is a must-do hunt if you are a waterfowl enthusiast. With slightly more than 2,000 licensed hunters, this resource seems practically untapped.

A Traveling Sportsman

The author, Al Brant (center) and Chad Syphers enjoyed an epic goose hunt in PEI.

Upon entering the island, nothing can prepare the first-time visitor for the beauty of the province. The deep red soil of the numerous farm fields is interrupted only by strips of thick forest and bright green fields of grass or crops. This is potato country and the farms are immaculately kept, a tribute to the pride that islanders have in their homes. These same potato fields, along with soybean crops, barley and a variety of other attractants also draw the geese in by the droves. The best hunting occurs where fields containing some form of feed are situated in close proximity to the ocean, so birds coming off the water can drop into a field and feed. The top outfitters lease these spots, and the right combination of properties can spell success for an outfitter and their clients.

My host for my past three trips to PEI was one of the largest outfitters but has now retired from guiding. David McLellan leased more than 20 fields, allowing him unrestricted access to some of the best Canada goose hunting territory on the island. In some locations, McLellan had comfortable pit blinds. In others, hedgerow blinds provided cover and comfort for the hunters. In spots where these permanent blinds can't be constructed, McLellan utilized lay-out blinds, a camouflage sleeping bag style blind that hides hunters as they lie on the ground and allows them to spring up and shoot from a sitting position.

Hunters shooting from pit blind surprise geese as they land in the fields.

The morning of my first goose hunt came quickly and I was up at 4:00 a.m. After a hearty breakfast, my party met with our guide. A storm was rolling in from the west and this was good news for us, as the geese would be moving off the water to feed. After a short drive, we were in one of the fields that our outfitter leased for exclusive hunting rights. Not only does this practice provide the farmer with financial support, it ensures the hunters of exclusive rights to prime areas.

We quickly got settled into one of the blinds. This particular blind was of the hedgerow variety, bisecting two fields. Our guide explained that if the weather got too brutal, we would move to a heated pit blind.

As dawn broke, I looked over the massive spread of decoys our guide had set out early in the morning. I quickly noted that some of the decoys were full body style and some were silhouette dekes. Some PEI goose guides use silhouettes to add realism to the flock as the geese pass overhead. These silhouettes definitely looked real, and for good reason, they were made from photos of real Canadas! Other guides on the island use even more realistic decoys locally called stuffers. Stuffers are actual geese that have been mounted by a taxidermist or knowledgeable guide. Special care goes into the storage and upkeep of these expensive dekes, but the results are amazing.

A stuffed goose decoys birds better than any manufactured decoy but requires special care.

Although the goose season in PEI typically runs from early October through early December, prime time is the beginning of October to early November. Hunters can bag five geese per day.

The island also offers ruffed grouse, grey partridge (Hungarian partridge) and duck hunting. Additionally, if conditions and time permit, most outfitters will guide hunters for those birds as well. On my last trip, we took the afternoon to hunt Hungarian partridge, also called Huns. These small, quail-like creatures set up in coveys and roam the dirt perimeter roads alongside fields, eating grain crops. By driving along the edge of the fields, you can see the coveys and walk up on them. As you approach, the birds will scatter into the hedge between the fields. By stepping into the hedge, you flush the birds in an explosion of wings as they scatter in all directions. If your senses are quick and your aim is true, you can down one or maybe two. If you miss, the birds only flush a dozen yards or so and can be located and flushed again. Hunters are allowed three Hungarian partridge, which don't come easily.

Rene Lavoie shows off the massive wingspan of a Canada goose.

McLellan and his guides also took my party out for sea ducks and puddle ducks, as requested. The island typically produces a cornucopia of waterfowl, featuring black ducks, mallards, pintails, teal, widgeon, old squaw and more. Hunting along the island shore, over grain fields or on an inland waterway will put hunters into ducks most any day of the season. Dave doesn't guide hunters anymore, but a strong contingent of guides work up in PEI, so it's just a matter of settling on one for your hunt. The rates were and still are reasonable. Keep in mind that prices are in Canadian funds, which fluctuate almost always in our favor, depending on the exchange rate. Prince Edward Island is a beautiful destination with some world-class hunting and breathtaking scenery.

Bahamian Snorkeling Adventure

Below the surface of the turquoise-colored water sat an old truck tire, partially covered by the white sand. Around the inner portion where the rim would have attached were six pairs of antennae, jutting out from inside the tire. The antennae moved slowly in the slight current. Occasionally, one of the spiny lobsters attached to the antennae would venture out, partially exposing enough of the body for me to spear. Timing this exposure was no easy task. In the clear Bahamian waters just off of Cable Beach, Nassau, what looked like 6' of depth turned out to be more than 15'. At first, holding my breath to be able to reach the bottom and safely return was a chore, but after several dives, I became accustomed to the strain on my lungs.

My first dive was a complete failure. I misjudged the trajectory of the spear and my shot went into the sand, sending the lobsters on a fast retreat to the safety of their tire. Drawing the spear, holding my breath and remaining submerged was a difficult proposition, to say the least. At least six more attempts were unsuccessful and I was beginning to think I wouldn't score on this trip. Granted I had a great day diving the reef and phenomenal luck diving for conch shells, but I was determined to harvest a lobster in the traditional Bahamian manner.

With lungs burning and muscles aching, I dove again. This time I hit the lobster, but I only nicked it, sending a piece of its shell to the ocean floor. In seconds, a dozen small fish were there to feed on the shell and harass the injured lobster. This would turn out to work in my favor. As the fish pecked at his injury, he came completely out of the tire in an attempt to flee the marauding fish. Taking a deep breath, I went into a dive while readying my spear. Drawing back on the tube, I released the spear when it was just inches from the lobster's back. I could feel the lobster kick through the steel spear as I took my prize to the surface. I was greeted with cheers from my boat mates, all who had tired from diving and were waiting for me to board the boat. It seems they had given up after a long day of shell collecting and snorkeling. I climbed aboard, exhausted, with a sunburnt back from hovering on the surface, but as thrilled with my small catch as I was after shooting my first deer. My lobster joined the four our guide, Captain Paul Wells on the Ninja Boat, would take home for dinner.

The Bahamas are made up of more than 700 islands situated in the heart of the Caribbean. Nassau is one of the more populated islands and the epicenter of the tourism industry, with beachfront resorts, casinos and shopping destinations. My trip was to the Breezes Resort, an all-inclusive vacation destination situated on the white sands of Cable Beach. I planned a 5-day stay to celebrate the end of summer and would have been content to sit on the beach all day and float in the warm waters, but having an adventuresome spirit, I decided to venture out on a snorkeling tour. Several boat captains walk Cable Beach hoping to get a group of tourists to join them on a snorkeling trip. Some of the guides use a high-pressure sales pitch and by the end of the day, you learn to ignore them along with the cigar hawkers, jewelry and clothing vendors, but there was something different about Captain Paul and his Ninja boat, so we climbed aboard the first day for a reef snorkeling trip.

After several dives, the author managed to spear his first spiny lobster in the crystal-clear waters off Nassau, Bahamas.

Captain Paul, a native Bahamian, specializes in taking small groups of four out to the reef, just minutes off Cable Beach. For $40.00 per person, Capt. Paul outfits you with sterilized snorkel gear, a brief safety class, and an introductory lesson in reef fish and then provides an unforgettable snorkeling adventure in arguably one of the world's most beautiful oceans.

His friendliness and enthusiasm are contagious and we quickly became good friends. On our first day, we wound our way along the surface where giant brain coral and a living reef teemed with exotic fish, rays and interesting marine life. Captain Paul broke up a few bagels and tossed them in the water after calling in the fish by banging on the side of his boat. Hundreds, if not thousands of fish, ranging in size from an inch or two up to large groupers made their way to the boat and tickled me as they swam by. The snorkeling was easy in this quiet water located less than one-half mile offshore. After several hours of swimming, I returned to the beach, singing the praises of Capt. Paul and his boat.

The next day, while visiting some of the local shops, I saw many large and beautiful conch shells. I spied Capt. Paul on the beach again and inquired about the possibility of a shelling trip. I was in luck, as some of the best shelling sat just across from where we were, on an island owned by Bob Marley's record producer, Chris Blackwell. We headed out with two gals from Ohio I met the previous night in the resort bar who were interested in the snorkeling tales I relayed the night before.

After an hour on the reef again, we then motored over to walk the shoreline of Blackwell's Island. The beautiful white sands hid the white sea biscuits, which are essentially plumped up sand dollars. We scooped up a few as souvenirs and continued on. In contrast, the Bahamas sea star, a giant reddish-orange starfish, stood out like a sore thumb. Bleeding tooth nerites, a small jagged edge snail, attaches itself to rocks and makes an interesting addition to any shell collection. Just be sure to immerse the nerites in cola for an hour or so to get the snail out, or else they will stink.

The starfish and shells were great, but we were after conch shells, so Captain Paul motored just off shore and anchored. On my first dive, I found a stunning brown and white shell with gorgeous smooth edges. I tossed it to Captain Paul who proudly exclaimed that I had found one of the most sought-after shells, the king helmet conch. These shells sell for $75 to $100 in the local markets, so I was rightly pleased. We also found several queen conch with their vivid pink inside surfaces that had once held the edible conch but had been harvested and returned to the ocean floor. After my lobster spearing experience, we were all exhausted and headed back to the beach, pleased with my treasures that would remind me of this trip for years to come.

Because Ninja is a licensed boat, its passengers can harvest conch and lobsters, but all diving has to be unaided by bottled oxygen. Visitors are allowed to bring back shells if they are free of their inhabitants and can take home starfish if they have been preserved. Captain Paul took care of our sea stars with a formalin injection and I paid a local $20 to extract the conch from my king helmet shell, a process which took the better part of 45 minutes and left the captain exhausted. He repeatedly threw the shell into the wet sand along the shoreline until the conch critter had enough and started to leave the shell.

This Bahamas adventure took place in early September, just before the official start of the hurricane season. Rates drop that month and a 4-night, 5-day stay at our all-inclusive resort, complete with airfare out of Portland, Maine, was only $800 per person. Aside from a brief shower each day, I was greeted with temperatures in the 90s. Snorkeling in the pristine waters of the Caribbean has spoiled me to Maine's waters, and I will undoubtedly go back to this part of the world again. With great rates, easy access and incredibly beautiful and abundant sea life, the Bahamas are just the ticket for the traveling sportsman.

These are but a few of my trips outside of Maine. In all instances, the company I kept was as enjoyable as the shooting or angling. As the saying goes, "There's no place like home," but I felt at home on each adventure and took a bit of the experience back to my sporting excursions in the Pine Tree State. I look forward to more horizon-broadening trips with abundant game or big fish. If not, I know where to find them just outside my door.

Boats and Motors

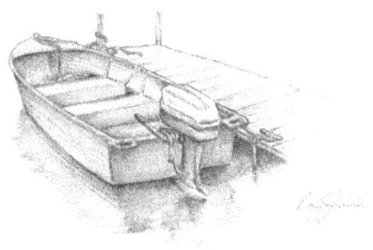

As a kid, I was fascinated with anything that had an engine. I also lived to fish, so it's no surprise that I was drawn to outboard motors early on. I would watch Dad pull a heavy outboard out from under the camp and screw it onto the transom of a wood or aluminum boat and before long, we were zooming across the lake on our way to a fishing spot.

Like any kid, I wanted to drive the vessel, and sometimes Dad would oblige and let me hold the tiller, albeit under a watchful eye. Eventually I would watch him start the motors, so I knew the sequence. Squeeze the primer bulb, pull out the choke, set the tiller handle to start and pull the cord. It looked so easy but yet so mystical. There were things like fresh sparkplugs, plug gaps, point settings, shear pins and the right oil ratio that I hadn't yet figured out.

As a youngster, I was allowed to row the boat out to fish by myself or with a friend, as long as I kept my lifejacket on. I got pretty good at rowing, but I wanted to man the controls. I would continually bug Dad to let me use the motor on my fishing ventures. An insurance man by trade, he knew every risk and bad outcome, so the answer was no. One day, when I asked him for the umpteenth time, he said when I was strong enough to start the motor by myself, I could take the boat out using the outboard.

Hot damn! This would be easy. I had watched him do it a hundred times. That next morning when we went out fishing, I asked, "Can I start it?" "Sure," he said, knowing the outcome. I gripped the starter handle and pulled for all I was worth. That thing wouldn't budge. Not to be outdone by a small outboard, I gave it the old two-handed grip and tried with both arms. I got a few inches out of the cord, but not enough to generate a spark. Looks like I was going to have to wait another year.

Jim and Tom's Adventure

That following year saw us at Rangeley Lake in an old rustic lodge with family friends. The Kluges had 2 boys and a girl. The younger boy, Jim, was a year younger than me, so he and I hung out. Our dads fished every morning and evening. Sometimes we went along, other times we stayed and roamed the woods around Rangeley Lake, certain we would locate a cache of old Indian artifacts.

One day I asked Dad if I could row Jim out to the middle of Greenvale Cove and fish. There were, and still are, some whopper yellow perch in the cove and that is sport enough for a pair of young boys. Jim and I climbed into the boat and I made a beeline for the shallow part of the cove.

We fished for probably an hour with no luck, so I started to row us back. As I neared the camp, the notorious Rangeley winds picked up and I found it increasingly harder to row. I could see Mom on the dock watching us, but I was steadily drifting backwards, despite my steady rowing pace. Next thing I know, Dad was running along the shoreline yelling at me to come to shore. I tried to turn the boat, but the wind was too strong. Finally, Dad had enough of this fun, so he slipped off his shoes and stepped into the lake and swam out to rescue us. He crawled aboard, no small feat for a middle-aged man, and fired up the motor, bringing us back to camp. My mom told that story often and she always remarked that I was rowing like the boat was on fire and Jim was calm at the front of the boat with extreme confidence in his captain.

The author, standing and saluting like Admiral Horatio Nelson, and Jim Kluge (in life jacket). John and Julie Kluge also spent time each summer with Tom and his family.

A few years later, Dad decided to buy his own outboard. We went to a marine shop somewhere and got a six-horsepower 1966 Evinrude Fisherman. This little motor was just the ticket to power the small aluminum boats that came with the cottages we rented. Sometimes Dad would throw the motor in the trunk and we would rent a boat for the day. I remember it was six bucks for half a day back then. Not a bad deal.

Dad soon tired of that, so he bought a used 12-foot aluminum boat. I was twelve at the time and could help him throw it on top of his Oldsmobile. Off we'd go on adventure after adventure. I could start the motor, so I did a lot of the piloting.

One day, while we were unloading the boat from the car top, my end slipped and the boat dinged his vinyl top. We headed out to buy a trailer that weekend. With a hitch installed on his trusty Oldsmobile, we were good to go. We had that rig for years and

Boats and Motors

when I was 22, he gave it to me and I ran it for a few years before upgrading. That setup served us well and we caught a lot of fish and chatted a ton between her gunwales.

I think I was 14 or so when I spent the summer at my grandfather's place. He owned a cement contracting business and I loved to go along to the job site and help out as best I could. He had a big basement where he stored many of his tools and I would go down there and build stuff. One day I found an old outboard under the stairs. I asked him about it and he said it was a Ward's five-horsepower model. It looked much older than my dad's 1966 model. Pa couldn't remember the year, but I think it was a late 40s model. I told him I wanted to get it running and so began my instruction in outboard mechanics.

Pa went through that engine and explained to me all the fundamentals: spark, compression, coils, etc. He showed me how to check for a spark, which it had. He mixed up some fresh gas, checked the lower unit fluid and we threw it in a trashcan full of water. Wouldn't you know, it fired right up and we had her running right. The next day we rented an old wooden boat and took it for a spin. Worked like a charm.

Now fast forward 40 years. I wish I still had that motor. Like a woman with a penchant for stylish shoes, I can't pass up a beautiful outboard. Many years ago, I picked up a folding three-horsepower Evinrude because I thought I'd someday have a square-stern canoe for duck hunting and it would push that perfectly. It sat in the back of Larry Higgins's shop, Higgins Sport Center, in Auburn. Larry was a great skeet shot and sold some fine shotguns and his son, Mike, worked on boats and motors out back. I struck a deal with Larry and I finally got the canoe, just 30 years later.

The canoe purchase included a six-horse Johnson Sea Horse. I found that to be a tad much for the canoe, but I haven't sold it or traded it away, yet. A few years back I was in an antique shop and I saw a gleaming vision amongst the detritus of the store. A 1958 Evinrude Lightwin in three-horsepower. It was even on a factory original Evinrude motor stand! After a small amount of haggling, I got both for a song. Aside from dried out coils, this thing was mint. I replaced the coils and guess what pushes my canoe now?

Tinkering

    Last summer I was walking on the camp road and I spied a pile of junk placed outside an old camp. There sat a 1966 Evinrude 18-horsepower Fastwin. What a classic motor. This is essentially a 20-horsepower motor and wouldn't it push a fishing boat around! It looks like a 1950s car with sleek, angled lines. Over the fall and winter, I rebuilt the carburetor, put in fresh coils, points and condensers and added a new set of plugs. She starts on the first pull and runs strong. I put a new 30-horse Mercury four-stroke on my fishing boat, so I have no need for the 18. It's probably time to sell or trade off a few of those motors, but I haven't found a consignment store for fishermen yet.

    Call me nostalgic, but I love those old motors. A sport could work on them with just a few basic tools and a little knowledge. Their shape and style takes me back to the early days of my fishing adventures. Those were certainly simpler times. Today I have electronics in my boat that weren't even thought of back then. I have a smart phone that will run my trolling motor, entertain me with a playlist of songs and check the weather for the next week. My downriggers track the bottom and adjust automatically if the depth changes. My fish finder plots my course by following the contour map of the lake I am on. These things do improve my catch rates, but I still go out on the dock with a bobber and night crawler at least once each year. Technology is good, but I'd trade it all for another trip in that old boat with Dad. And this time I'm positive I could start the motor on my own.

Counting Boats

    How many boats does one outdoorsman or woman need? That is a loaded question. Can one boat cover all of your hunting and fishing needs? I'd have to answer no on that one. An old guide

Boats and Motors

I know once told me that any boat is a compromise. Sage words from an experienced skipper. It would be hard to have the perfect boat unless you fished for just one fish in one manner and never did anything else.

My first craft was a canoe. It was 1988 and I was graduating from the University of Maine at Orono. My parents asked me what I would like for a graduation gift. The choice was obvious: a new Old Town canoe. I was fortunate that our campus was right near the Old Town factory and I had been by to see all the beautiful models they had. I was also fortunate that the UMO Outing Club let us borrow canoes whenever we wanted, so my mind was set on a sturdy but lightweight Old Town.

Come graduation day we headed over to the factory, still at the original location back then and went inside. The salesman asked what I would use it for and I told him: duck hunting, trout fishing and general exploring. Using an old salesman's line, he said "You're in luck today. I have just the thing."

He led us away from the shiny new canoes into a room of "scratch and dent" specials. There sat a Pathfinder model, just shy of 15 feet. It was a dark green inside and out, perfect for duck hunting. He told me it was a factory sample as they wanted to see what that model looked like with the dark green coloration. It had a few scratches from being shoved around, but I would add plenty more, so that didn't bother me a bit. The salesman said it was only $250 because it was a sample. They ran it down the old wooden chute that led to the parking lot and I had it lashed down on my 1979 International Scout II in no time at all. I use this canoe every duck season and also for trout fishing or just exploring lakes and ponds. I've also transported deer in it that I shot in marshes or by rivers. So, I guess a canoe is definitely on the list.

One of my most recent vessel acquisitions is that square-stern canoe. Why would anyone need a second canoe, you ask? Well, it all started with a motor. I have that beautiful 1958 Evinrude 3-horse motor that runs like a top, but I needed a small boat to put it on. I also like to fish a few small ponds that are hard to get into with my aluminum boat (more about her soon), so I had my eyes

Boats and Motors

open for a square-stern canoe for some time. Sure, I'd love an old Rangeley boat or a Grand Laker, but wooden boats are a lot of upkeep and the Lakers are too costly. Old Town made an economical 17-foot square-stern canoe, the Discovery Sport Boat, so I hunted for one of those. After all, I could duck hunt out of that, too and it comes with oars, so it could function as a sculling boat. I'm just convincing myself here. Feel free to use this argument with your spouse if you find yourself in the same proverbial waters. Well, I found a Sport Boat and the rest is history.

Now you've heard me talk about ice-out trolling on Sebago and Rangeley Lakes. Those lakes demand a stable boat that can handle a chop. A Maine angler needs a good deep vee hull boat to stay safe and secure, so of course I have an 18-foot deep vee aluminum boat for all of my angling needs. My boat of choice is a Starweld. This all-welded baby is powered by a 90-horsepower Honda outboard and has an 80-pound Minn Kota Ulterra trolling motor. It does all I need, where I need it. I guide out of her and although it's smaller than what most guides run, this boat is all business and set up to catch fish in what I call an intimate manner. She's even named the "Black Ghost" after the famous fly originated by artist, guide and taxidermist Herbert Welch of Rangeley. You will see a few of these boats on Maine lakes, along with some other solid brands like the Lund, Princecraft and Tracker products. If you want to stay on the water in windy days, get a nice, deep, wide aluminum boat. You won't regret it.

And what do we do when it's too hot to fish at the lake? We go tubing, or water skiing or just cruising, so of course you need a boat for that. I have a 21-foot Four Winns with a big 302-cubic inch inboard that has been in the family since 1993. It may be a tad oxidized and faded, but my kids learned all about Sebago Lake on that boat and she still starts and runs each year.

So, like the owl said when asked about how many licks it took to get to the center of a Tootsie Pop, the answer is four. You need four boats to do it all!

At Camp

If you spend any time pursuing this sporting life, invariably you will find yourself in some form of camp. For any of you from other parts of the country, a camp in Maine could be a shack, a cottage or a million-dollar home on a lake. All that is required to achieve the camp moniker is that it is away from your home. Maine comedian Bob Marley has a whole shtick on this phenomenon in his Upta Camp monologue. He nails it, describing things like the stiff towels that wouldn't cut it at home, so they are brought to camp.

My mom, originally a Midwesterner, never embraced the term. The place on Sebago Lake where they enjoyed their retirement and where I now live was a year-round home, so she cringed when I or anyone else called it a camp. But more about that camp later.

I can honestly say that I never spent time in a camp that I didn't like. Perhaps it is because any time in a camp is time away from work and other similar encumbrances. I rank camps by superlatives. The oldest, the most primitive, the fanciest. Let's start with the oldest.

At Camp

The camp we rented on Rangeley Lake when I was a youngster was one of the early camps on the lake. It was situated above the shore of the lake with other smaller, but similarly constructed dwellings around it. Our camp was the main lodge. It still had the huge fireplace that us kids could stand up in. Mom was impressed with the kitchen table. It seated more than a dozen. Clearly the sports would gather there three times a day for their repast. Once satiated, they would amble back to their small cottages to head out fishing, nap or sleep until the next day.

The camp that the author and his family stayed at on Rangeley Lake still stands.

I recall the big rock along the shoreline and a birch tree growing out of a crack in the rock. The western shore of Rangeley Lake is covered in birch trees, and nothing conjures up memories of that region like the paper birch. There was a caribou shoulder mount on the wall in the living area, an ancient mount. The animal had spindly antlers, so I suspect it could have been a Maine caribou. The last caribou taken in Maine was shot in 1908. That camp

At Camp

is still there, still wearing its deep red color and as I troll by it each spring, I wonder who owns it now.

Perhaps the most primitive camp I stayed at was the caribou camp in northern Quebec. This spot was carved out of the tundra by flying supplies in on float planes in good weather. The camps themselves were not much. Wood decks support two-by-four walls covered in plywood and topped with a blue tarp. A small woodstove provided enough heat to be comfortable. The temperature at caribou camp could be in the teens at night and 65 degrees during the day, with wind, rain and snow appearing randomly. While rustic, this was home for a week.

The coldest camp I was in was located in Baxter State Park and I stayed there one January. While I was at the University of Maine, the wildlife program held a Winter Ecology class in January. We came back to school early from winter break and were in for quite an experience. To begin with, we had to cross-country ski into the rough log cabins about 12 miles on unplowed roads. Each day we would sojourn out on snowshoes to study moose droppings, snow depth and other interesting topics. The conditions were brutal, but the camaraderie and lessons made us almost forget the sub-zero temperatures. Almost.

Some of the best-equipped camps I have stayed at have been the camps that L.L. Bean owns in Oquossoc on Rangeley Lake which are rented out to employees. With Rene working for L.L. Bean, we had access to these camps for moose, bird and fishing seasons. Of course, they had L.L. Bean furnishings galore. Because they are rented out, they did not allow dogs on the property. I often commented to Rene that old Leon Bean would be rolling over in his grave if he knew that hunting dogs weren't allowed in his camps.

One of the camps I frequented the most belonged to Dick Small, former Auburn police chief. It was located in Stratton in the heart of some great bird hunting. Some people are stingy with their camps, rarely inviting guests or allowing others to use it when the owners are away. Others are generous, wanting friends to experience the same joys that they do. Dick was generous, and Rene

At Camp

and I spent most Octobers and some Novembers at his rustic camp. Apparently, the cabin originally belonged to a thief who would steal firewood from the neighbors. Dick told me that one neighbor had his fill of the pilfering, so he drilled a hole in a log and put a stick of dynamite inside the firewood. Dick showed me the portion of wall where the stove sat and it was newer than the rest of the camp. One day he apparently chose a loaded log and it blew the stove out of the camp. I'm not sure if that story was true, but it's one hell of a tale.

One way to keep getting invited back to camp is by pitching in with chores or when maintenance is needed. I cut a lot of firewood to heat my first house, so I always brought a truckload up for Dick to use. One fall, Dick re-covered the camp in plywood, so I came up and stained the camp for him. We took a lot of birds in the Eustis-Stratton area from that camp, so I never minded chipping in.

Back to the family "camp" at Sebago Lake. This is my home base now. Dad always wanted to retire on a lake and he achieved his goal. He also wanted my family to enjoy the same option. Mom loved a full house and kids and friends were always welcomed. I've made a few updates, but the big fireplace still occupies most of the living room. As I write these lines, I have the old floor lamp Dad used to keep on his screened-in porch. He read the newspaper underneath its yellow glow after supper, sometimes with a cigar, when the wind was right. An old coffee cup, a wooden loon carving and a few other odds and ends remind me of earlier times here with my parents.

There is an ancient birch tree down by the dock, similar to the one at Rangeley Lake. This one, too, grows from a shoreside rock, and has been there for decades. Dad was concerned that it would fall into the lake and, although it is leaning that way, it hasn't yet. Dad was always after me to trim it. He said he wanted a better view of the lake. I think he wanted it trimmed to lessen the chance it would topple.

Not far from the birch tree is a bench near the water's edge. This is Bette's bench. Mom would sit there and watch the kids splashing in the lake or Dad fishing from the dock. As age got the better of her, it was easier to sit there than navigate the dock or beach, so she was content to call that her spot.

    Camp conjures up different images for all of us who have spent time there. It can be as relaxing as a lazy summer day or as quiet as a winter night. Camp life, no matter how opulent or rustic, is celebrated, sought after and missed. Until you visit again.

On Dogs

Noted wildlife photographer and longtime announcer at the Westminster Kennel Club Dog Show, Roger Caras, said, "Dogs aren't our whole life, but they make our lives whole." No words rang truer for a sport. Bird hunts without the aid of a canine can't be compared to one with a well-trained pointer, flusher or retriever. Paddling out to get your duck is not as enjoyable as sending a headstrong Lab into the marsh.

Rene, with his New England wit and wisdom, commented when I put my first Lab down, "That's the problem with dogs—they just don't live long enough." It's been said that a hunter will own three dogs in his or her lifetime, given the 10- to 12-year lifespan of a hunting dog. Not enough, in my opinion.

I've had the pleasure of owning one good hunting dog and spent some time with one good dog that hunts. I've also had the enjoyment of hunting over many other excellent sporting dogs. Rene and I shot over some solid bird dogs on those guided hunts in New Brunswick. Brownie was a German shorthair that was like radar on the province's abundant grouse and woodcock. Nothing like walking up on a rock-solid point, knowing that a flush is imminent.

Our guide, Earl, also employed the aid of a springer spaniel. I can't remember her name, but Rene and I laugh about her all the time. The first time her handler let her out, she raced back and forth in front of us. When she passed us, she would spring into the air and look us in the eyes, as her breed name implies. She was good on birds, too, but awful silly to watch.

I had the best deal ever on a bird dog. My friend, Adam Farrington, had a sweet German shorthair named Parker who took a liking to my youngest daughter, Olivia. Parker would have play dates with Olivia and his mild demeanor changed how I thought about the normally rambunctious breed. It wasn't long before Adam was allowing me to "rent" Parker out for bird hunts. Adam knew I was good with dogs, but the highest level of trust one sportsman can bestow on another is to allow you to hunt their dog. Adam was busy with work and Parker needed the exercise, so we shot a number of pheasant and grouse over his points.

Now Adam has a new dog, Rylee, a brown shorthair. I picked her up this fall to do some real bird hunting over her and we hit it off like sweethearts. The first night before the big hunt above Rangeley she hopped up on my bed and spent the night pressed against my side. She took to Rene immediately, too, sprawling across his lap on the ride to and from our hunting grounds. After seeing how much potential and instinct she had, plus feeling her warmth during the ride, Rene remarked, "we're going to have some good years with her coming up." That made me smile for many reasons.

Parker was old when the author borrowed him to hunt but he was a solid pointer and a sweet soul.

    Turner sat curled up at my feet while I penned many of these chapters. Of all the dogs I've known, I never met one with so much gentleness and soul in his eyes. Goldens are known for their disposition, but this boy is something special. Loyal, playful and with a hint of stubbornness. Very much like someone else I know.

    I wish Turner could have met Luke. Perhaps they would compare notes about me. Luke could offer up tips on getting an extra snack. Turner could ask how many times he needed to bark until I would let him out.

The author and Turner, the most gentle dog ever.

I was at an auction to benefit the Lucky Pup Rescue group, an organization that works to get dogs out of shelters and into homes before they are euthanized. I saw a great painting by Maine artist Katie Maloney of two yellow labs holding a stick and coming out of a lake. I bid and won the painting and I had a stroke of genius. Maloney was at the auction, so I asked her if I could commission her to modify the artwork to feature an aged chocolate Lab and a young golden retriever. I explained that I could see my old Lab, Luke, "passing the stick" to the new dog, Turner. He would be telling Turner to take good care of the family. She loved the idea and after seeing some photos of both dogs, had the work finished. It proudly hangs on the wall facing the lake, where both dogs have enjoyed many summers.

Nothing adds to our sport like a good dog, but when you think about it, how many times does a bird dog get to hunt in a year? The most die-hard hunters will hit the woods every day from October through December. Most of us only get out a handful of times. So that hunting dog, in reality, is a family dog that hunts. But, like most of you, I would take my dog ice fishing, trolling and just plain exploring, too. Most times it's at his urging because he just wants to go along. You can't ask for more loyalty than that.

The Big Lake

Most of us who spend time on the water fall into one of two classifications: lake people, or ocean people. Sure, there are some anadromous folks who spend time on both kinds of water, but generally we choose a path. For certain I put my time in on salt water, whether it was sailing, fishing for stripers, surf casting for pompano and jack in Florida or just enjoying the salty breeze of a beach. But, if I had to choose one vocation, it would be freshwater.

Some of us were summer kids, arriving at the lake for the joyous carefree months of warm weather and few responsibilities. Others may have grown up living on a lake, not paying it much attention. Still others, the most appreciative lot, got on the water when they could and made the most of fleeting moments.

I've had the pleasure of enjoying many lakes, beginning as a toddler. I caught my first fish, drove the boat by myself, even had my first kiss at a camp on the water. My dad loved the water and loved to fish, so it was inevitable that we would end up at some lake somewhere, at first for a week, then a longer trip, then the better part of a lifetime on Sebago Lake. For this angler, Sebago Lake is home base and has been for decades.

The woods surrounding Sebago Lake were first inhabited by Native Americans. The Rockameecook branch of the Sokokis or Pequawket tribe named the lake Sebago, translated to "great stretch of water" or, simply, "big lake." Sebago comes by that name honestly and although it's the state's second largest lake (to Moosehead Lake), it is the deepest, at more than 300 feet deep. This deep, clear water is one reason why the lake is the drinking source for all of greater Portland.

For anglers, Sebago holds more mystique, being the home of the world-record landlocked salmon. In 1907, Edward Blakely of Darien, Connecticut, dredged up a 38-inch monster. It has been said that larger fish were taken by anglers who cared little for trophy status, preferring the flesh of the fish over any record. This was the heyday of Maine angling heritage. Sports from away came up on trains and stayed at grand inns and hotels. While the salmon don't run that big anymore, slot limits of lake trout are producing some 20-pound whoppers and there is still an abundance of salmon to be had, especially at ice-out.

As sporting and often as serene as Sebago Lake is, it is a big body of water and it can get ugly. Each summer, it seems a thunderstorm rolls through and whips the lake up into a frenzy. The summer of 2018 I was caught in such a storm, the roughest I've ever seen the lake and it gave me a new respect for this body of water.

Rough Water

It was the end of July and I had guests at the lake. Bryan Gilliard, the Chief of Police in Monroe, North Carolina, and his wife Crystal met me in Quebec at a training conference and I wanted to show them Maine. The weather called for a storm that evening, so an afternoon trip up the Songo River should have been safe.

The Songo River empties Long Lake and Brandy Pond from the north into Sebago Lake. One of the most interesting features of the river is the lock system. This structure is the last surviving of 28 locks built in the 1800s that allowed commercial barges to go from Portland harbor to Harrison. It's a great experience for visitors to see the lock function. The locks attendant motions for boaters to enter and stack up in the narrow structure. They then close the gate of the lock by pushing a large lever with back and leg power. Once the gate is closed, they turn the water gear to fill or drain the locks, depending on the direction of travel of the boaters. Boaters coming down from Brandy Pond need to drop 5 feet to get into Sebago Lake. The locks accomplish that feat.

We took a leisurely boat ride across the lake, up the Songo River and went through the locks. Once we passed through Brandy Pond, we went under the bridge at the Naples Causeway and entered Long Lake. I tied up at the public dock and we ate lunch at one of the lakeside spots. It was a beautiful day, so we headed over to the dock where pilot Matthew McFadden has his float plane tied up. I wanted to show Bryan and Crystal the lake from the air, so off we went. I commented on the dark clouds to our west and Matt said they wouldn't be arriving for a few hours, so we should be safe for the boat ride home. We motored over the house and saw some of the other sights on the lake and landed in Naples. As I motored down Brandy Pond I saw Matt take off with another flight tour, so I felt we were good, weather-wise.

Once we got through the locks, the wind was really picking up. Although we were sheltered by the tree-lined river, the wind was getting past the trees. As we rounded the last bend and came up to the mouth of the lake, it was evident there was a huge windstorm moving across the lake. The waves looked like four-footers from where I was. The only boat in sight was a pontoon boat and he pulled up to the sand bar, beaching his boat. I contemplated doing that, too, but didn't feel our anchor would keep us there in this wind. It was ferocious. I made the decision to cross the lake slowly. I told Bryan and Crystal that it would be a bumpy ride, but we would take it easy. My big boat is a 21-foot bowrider with a deep hull. I steered her into the wind to slice at the waves head on. They were big. I thought they were the biggest I had ever seen

The Big Lake

on Sebago. The hull was doing what it was meant to, slicing the waves and pushing them to each side of the boat.

As we got out into the middle of the lake, the boat was riding up and down in the wave cycle. Quickly the 21-foot boat became small. I had to motor up into the oncoming roller and then crash down off its backside. This was ocean boating, not a lake cruise. All of a sudden, a big wave crested over the boat and I yelled "Hold on!" That was enough for me, and I'm certain for Bryan and Crystal. I hollered over the storm to Bryan to get the life jackets out and on. I put mine on once theirs were secure. A pleasant day had gone from a challenging trip across rough water to survival mode. I made sure the bilge pump was on because if the boat stalled, we faced being swamped. I turned the boat away from the wind and headed for the nearest shore. I told my now-frightened passengers that we were going to head for shore and find a dock or mooring to tie onto. I cautioned Bryan that the shore was close by, so we may have only one chance to get secured to something.

I could see a free dock along the eastern shore, so we made for that. I told Bryan to get a rope ready, but cautioned him to keep his fingers out of any shackles or cleats as this wind would rip them off if they got caught. Bryan was not impressed with my directions. As we neared the dock, the homeowner was watching our plight from his rain-sheeted window. He hollered that we could tie up. I spotted a large mooring ball and decided that would be safer. Bryan was ready and had us tied onto the bow cleat in quick order. We spun quickly into the wind and despite the fierce storm, we were safe.

In a matter of minutes, it was over. The storm passed through. The lake became calm again, calm enough to head home. I could still see some more black clouds, so I put the throttle all the way forward and beat feet for home base. We were tied up at the dock just in time for the second deluge, which we watched from inside the camp. We were soaked and a bit worse for the wear. Bryan said in his southern drawl, "I haven't been in a boat since I was eight years old." Not sure if he wants to do so again.

I always respect the water, but I gained a newfound respect for Sebago Lake on that day. I replayed the decisions in my head. Should I have beached the boat on the sand bar? I still think we would not have held in that wind and I could have lost the boat. Knowing we were in danger and heading toward shore was my safest move. I'm glad I didn't try to push onward. It all turned out fine, and we laughed about the adventure over cocktails that night.

The big lake has provided fond memories, great angling and fun adventures for me and my family over the years. I'm fortunate to have lived along its shoreline and to have had such easy access to all it offers during every season. Now I guide on the lake and introduce others to its beauty and bounty. The big lake always has, and always will, hold a special spot in my heart.

Tidying Up

This has been a grand journey for me, searching back in my memory for tips, stories and happenings and I enjoyed having you along for the trek. It caused me to wrack my brain to remember a year or an age when something took place. I had to phone old friends to get their help with an elusive answer. I pored over old photos, some of which I selected to illustrate these chapters, while others just brought me familiar comfort.

These pages forced me to focus on content, word choice and organization. In doing so, I reflected upon so many years of adventures. When I wrote about my dogs, I went back to those proud moments when training paid dividends. But like all memories, some of those not-so-proud moments came back. If my math is correct, the good outweighed the bad and I wouldn't trade any of them away.

Likewise, when describing a shot taken, I thought back to the guns that have occupied space in my gun cabinet, closet or wall. My most-used bird gun is a 20-gauge Ruger Red Label. I shot a ton of grouse, a few woodcock and several pheasants with that

Tidying Up

gun. It's worn on the barrel end from rubbing on my boot when it rests on my lap while road hunting. It came by that wear honestly, and I wouldn't think of having it re-blued.

Those two guns my grandfather gave me are stowed in the cabinet now, but they delivered a lot of sport for me in my young days. Another gun that only comes out on clear weather days was given to me by my good friend and hunting partner. I cherish that gun as I cherish our friendship. For some reason, my deer rifles don't hold any sentimental value to me. I view them as tools. I can't figure that out, but it's how my brain works.

While this book proved to be reflective for me, my goal was to entertain you, the reader. Like telling a tale by the campfire, I wanted to share some of the enjoyable aspects of a sporting life with those of similar mindset and perhaps some who have never stepped into my woods or fished my waters. I also wanted to pass along the tips and tactics I learned from some very generous mentors and friends. We are too small a fraternity not to share. Outside attacks on our lifestyle seem to come harder and stronger reach year.

Each month brings us something different to do in this cornucopia state. I've touched upon a few topics that hold my interest. I hope that my choices interested you as well. It took us a whole year to get here, but time goes by quickly, then it all starts over again. It's ice fishing season and I haven't even replaced my leaders from last year. I need to change the lower unit fluid in the outboard because ice-out will be any day now. I better make sure the dog loses a few pounds before October gets here. Like a woodcock exploding from the floor of an alder run, these moments come and go so quickly within a sporting year in Maine.

About the Author

Tom Roth has been hooked on the outdoors ever since he caught his first fish at 18 months under the watchful eye of his grandfather. During his school years he longed to be outdoors and his parents thankfully accommodated his desires, renting camps and cabins in Maine, New Hampshire and Wisconsin before establishing a summer home on the shores of Sebago Lake. As a college student studying wildlife biology at the University of Maine, he sought out like-minded friends and escaped to the woods and waters between classes. Tom enjoyed a 32-year law enforcement career working as a summer game warden, a part-time deputy sheriff, a patrol officer, school resource officer, and even an undercover officer while working his way up the ranks and retiring once and jumping back into the work scene, now running Maine's Fraud Investigation Unit. Despite a full week of work, Tom spends as many hours afield or on the water as he can, be it hunting, fishing, boating, snowmobiling, skiing or just enjoying the beautiful State of Maine. His sporting adventures have taken him across the country, to Canada and the Caribbean. Since 1995, Tom has penned a regional column in *The Maine Sportsman*, New England's largest outdoor publication. Tom has also had thousands of articles published in national magazines. Tom now lives in the family home on Sebago Lake and guides anglers for the abundant lake trout and salmon that inhabit Maine's deepest lake on his boat, the "Black Ghost." His YouTube channel, Troth1966 and web page, www.sebagolakeguideservices.com highlight many of his adventures just as they happen—real, genuine and with no edits; the same way Tom enjoys living his life.

www.ingramcontent.com/pod-product-compliance
Lightning Source LLC
Chambersburg PA
CBHW051606170426
43196CB00038B/2945